STO

**ACPL ITEM
DISCARDED**

1.4.78

Birds of the Air

Also by Eric Simms

Bird Migrants
The Songs and Calls of British Birds
Voices of the Wild
Woodland Birds
Wild Life in the Royal Parks
Birds of Town and Suburb
Live and Let Live

With Myles North

Witherby's Sound Guide to British Birds

Birds of the Air

The autobiography of a
naturalist and broadcaster

Eric Simms

HUTCHINSON OF LONDON

Hutchinson & Co (Publishers) Ltd
3 Fitzroy Square, London W1

London Melbourne Sydney Auckland
Wellington Johannesburg and agencies
throughout the world

First published 1976
© Eric Simms 1976

Set in Monotype Garamond
Printed in Great Britain by The Anchor Press Ltd
and bound by Wm Brendon & Son Ltd
both of Tiptree, Essex

ISBN 0 09 126070 1

To Thelma

Who has shared and enriched
this story beyond all measure

2018698

'If a man love the labour of any trade, apart from any question of success and fame, the gods have called him.'

Robert Louis Stevenson

Contents

	Author's Preface	11
1	'On a Green Light!'	13
2	Origins and Beginnings	16
3	Oxford in Wartime	27
4	Call-Up	35
5	Flame Vines and Spanish Moss	42
6	From the Deep South to the Great Lakes	49
7	The War Comes Closer	56
8	The Air Assault on Europe	64
9	Pedagogy	81
10	Stalking Wildlife with a Microphone	88
11	Nature on the Air	108
12	Abroad for Birds	114
13	Television	124
14	Film-Making	132
15	Dollis Hill	140
16	African Safari	146
17	Wildlife on the World Service	164
18	Broadcasting House	170
19	Backwards and Forwards	177
	Chronology	184
	Index	187

Illustrations

Between pages 48 and 49

Aged three with my mother, Thomas, Wilfrid and Margaret, 1924 (*L. Simms*)

With my mother, Thelma and father at Badby, 1950 (*Stanley Wood*)

The Cottage, Ladbroke Square, 1934

With three friends on top of the Empire State Building, 1942

Wedding day, 23 December 1943 (*Tudor Press*)

The crew of Q-Queenie 2, 626 Squadron, Wickenby, 1944 (*Crown Copyright*)

Photograph I took of Essen, 26 April 1944 (*Crown Copyright*)

Setting up a three-foot diameter parabolic reflector. Buckinghamshire, 1957 (*BBC Copyright*)

Operating an 18-inch reflector in our portable boat. Buckinghamshire, 1957 (*BBC Copyright*)

Stone curlew at nest (*Eric Hosking*)

Hen golden eagle feeding eaglet (*Niall Rankin*)

Siamese kittens being recorded for a radio play, 1954 (*Mirrorpic*)

Badgers feeding in front of parabolic microphone. Surrey, 1953 (*Peter Bayly*)

With Thelma, Joan and George Burton, 1954

The Hilbre Group, 1957 (*London Press Photos*)

Percy Thrower showing how to make a miniature garden, January 1961 (*BBC Copyright*)

With the late James Fisher, April 1958 (*BBC Copyright*)

Illustrations

Between pages *112* and *113*

Carrying film equipment into the Caledonian Forest, 1959 (*F. R. Elwell*)

Thelma, David and Amanda, 1974 (*Stanmore Studios*)

On location at Great Tew for *A Year in the Country*, 1961 (*F. R. Elwell*)

Near the summit of Sgoran Dubh Mor in the Cairngorm Mountains, 1963 (*Charles Lagus*)

Dr Roger Bannister demonstrating cardiac output, 1965 (*BBC Copyright*)

The late Maxwell Knight introducing Rufus Creed and his tame vixen, 1961 (*BBC Copyright*)

Black rhinoceros and calf in Ngorongoro Crater (*Eric Hosking*)

Murchison Falls in Uganda, 1965 (*Eric Simms*)

Scene on the River Nile near Paraa, 1965 (*Eric Simms*)

Hippopotamus on a Nile mudbank, 1965 (*Eric Simms*)

Outdoor sound location shooting at Rob Roy's cottage, Glen Shira, 1970 (*F. R. Elwell*)

Indoor filming in the BBC News Studio in Broadcasting House, 1965 (*BBC Copyright*)

Filming *The Sands of Dee*, 1966 (*Hoylake News and Advertiser*)

On a Breton oysterboat returning from the island of Gavrinis, 1971 (*F. R. Elwell*)

Interviewing Sir Peter Scott for *Nature Notebook*, Bush House, 1968 (*BBC Copyright*)

Being interviewed for *The Living World* on the wildlife of Neasden. The Welsh Harp, 1972 (*Middlesex County Press*)

Author's Preface

I regard myself as a singularly fortunate man, having been able to turn what was my schoolboy hobby into my life's work. This has brought me a deeply treasured sense of fulfilment but not, I hope, too great an air of complacency! I have been able to travel, write, broadcast and devise radio and television programmes about wildlife for more than a quarter of a century. In these varied and stimulating activities I owe a very great debt to the British Broadcasting Corporation which has employed me both as a staff member and a freelance for most of my working life.

These autobiographical reminiscences are also the story of many other broadcasters, BBC colleagues and naturalists with whom I have been privileged to work. I am very grateful to all of them for their patience and for the advice and practical help which they so generously gave to me. I am also indebted to the BBC for permission to reproduce a number of pictures from their Photographic Library. My old friends Felicia Elwell, Eric Hosking and Charles Lagus have also kindly allowed me to reproduce some of their fine photographs.

I would also like to express my gratitude to Putnam and Company for their approval to my retelling some of the stories that were first published in my book *Voices of the Wild* and none, in fact, are reproduced verbatim. I have regularly kept notes and diaries but I wish to thank my brother Wilfrid – the family historian – for information that I have used in Chapter 2. I must also record my appreciation of the sympathetic and courteous way in which Gerald Austin has watched over this book on behalf of the publishers.

Much of this story is also that of my wife. She has cheerfully

Author's Preface

borne the separations and responsibilities occasioned by my long absences on field expeditions, especially when our children were young. She has helped me immeasurably, not only with her loyal and lasting support, but also with her valuable criticism of my writings and with her ability to recall events when my own memory proved uncertain.

Writers have advanced many reasons for embarking on their autobiographies. In my case several of my professional colleagues suggested that, because of the varied and interesting life that they believed I was leading, I should write my own. A good number have expressed a certain envy of my life style. This has served to reinforce my gratitude to the Fates which have made it possible, not only by granting me the opportunities in life, but also by giving me the wisdom to recognize them when they arose. Some readers may wish that more space had been devoted to wildlife in this book while others may regret the amount given to my personal attitudes and impressions. In fact, the more detailed accounts of my researches into natural history have appeared in earlier books and scientific papers. It is my sincere hope, however, that among the words and phrases in this book some readers will be able to share with me the wonder and sense of privilege that I have experienced from being on this earth and the inspiration that I have derived from the living creatures that inhabit it.

E.S.

I

'On a Green Light!'

'Will you go ahead, please, in ten seconds from now? On a green light!' From a discreetly concealed loudspeaker in the wall of the room where I am sitting come the soft instructions. I glance around. In front of me is an oblong table whose top is formed from a perforated metal grille set in a white formica frame. A heart-shaped microphone in a bronze-coloured housing hangs on elastic bands just sixteen inches from my mouth. On the table is a small tray with glasses and a jug holding some insipid water of uncertain age. At my side is a double-glazed window through which I can see into a cubicle where the producer and pretty studio manager are sitting at a control panel. Next to them are the producer's secretary, pouring over a clipboard and with one finger poised on a stop watch, and a second studio manager who is standing between two tape machines. Above the window is a row of three lights – white for telephone, blue for rehearsal and red for transmission or record. And the red bulb shines out unwinkingly. Just below it is a large electric clock gently but audibly thudding away the seconds. I settle myself, grasp the sheets of my script and take a deep breath.

Suddenly a green light on the table comes on, and I begin to read.

'All my life it's been my ambition to visit a breeding colony of flamingoes in Europe – to see those extraordinary Alice-in-Wonderland birds on their nesting island. Well, that great spectacle was granted to me when I stood some years ago on the sandy shore of a lagoon in the Camargue in southern France – that mysterious land of wild bulls, white horses and exotic birds. In the distance I could see through my field glasses an islet of pinkish white which shimmered and danced in the heat haze. It was a solid mass of flamingoes. Some were sitting on their nests and others just standing about in the shallow water. Here was a sight that only a bare handful of Englishmen had ever seen. There were no boats or punts on this lagoon and the only way that I would be able to reach the island would be by wading to it through the water. Henri Lomont, the chief warden of the Camargue wildlife sanctuaries, thought that the depth was between three and three and a half feet. As I looked across the lagoon I hoped that he was right!

'I had to carry a tape recorder, microphones and tapes safely through the water while Lomont's assistant volunteered to take the parabolic reflector that I used with my microphone to record birds at a greater distance. The floor of the lagoon was slippery with thick mud at the start and the going was bad. As the water grew deeper the bottom became firm and sandy and for the first half-mile we progressed at a steady pace. Then I noticed that tiny waves were beginning to lap the upper part of my chest, and the recorder, which I was carrying above my head, began to get heavier and heavier. The sun poured down on us from a brilliant blue sky and the water was cool but not unpleasant.

'As I waded slowly through quite deep water, the size of the flamingo colony began to reveal itself. A great phalanx of birds was spread before my eyes and I was able for the first time to hear the goose-like gobbling and honking calls. At last the water became more shallow and we moved round to the end of the island where there were fewest birds. In that way we wouldn't disturb them too much. The calls of the flamingoes were now loud and harsh, the nearer ones superimposed on the background chorus. Birds were flying low over our heads in a series of white, black and scarlet flashes. With long outstretched necks and trailing legs they looked like giant flying matchsticks – but to me they were superb in the air.

'I stood and gazed on this fantastic spectacle. Three thousand pairs of birds were tightly packed along a strip of land about three hundred yards long and some fifty yards wide. A few flamingos were striding about in the lagoon but most of them

'On a Green Light!'

were sitting on their inverted-flower-pot nests, with their legs folded back like giant pink safety pins, or standing tall, waving and flashing their half-opened wings like scarlet banners. I began to crawl towards the colony with my recording equipment until I was only eighty yards away. I put up the reflector and recorded two minutes of the huge chorus of sound. I crept forward again and this time a few of the great birds rose up from their nests and with great dignity walked down into the water. At thirty yards they stopped and waited in a queue until I had revealed my intentions. When I was within thirty feet of the nearest nests, I put the reflector on its tripod, connected up the microphone cable and walked back with forty yards of cable to a little clump of salicornia bushes.

'In a very few minutes the stately flamingoes began to move back to their mud nests and started to call right in front of the microphone. I could hear vibrant ringing "Ar-honks", high repeated "Kuk-kuk-kuks" and soft, conversational "Ker-wuks".'

(Here the studio manager plays in the relevant sound recording into the programme.)

That was an account of the way in which I made the first recordings in Europe of these magnificent birds and I only have to play them back to recapture at once that glorious summer day in the Camargue. Such a broadcast was made possible only by the British Broadcasting Corporation which had appointed me in 1950 to direct the Corporation's natural history recording projects. From this pioneering work I then moved into television production and film directing and finally became a freelance broadcaster and writer, but the BBC sound studio has remained very much my 'ecological niche'.

2

Origins and Beginnings

The summer of 1921 was long and hot. For my mother, who was small in stature with the figure of a young girl, it must have been a welcome relief when I was finally born on 24 August, two weeks overdue and well over ten pounds in weight. So I, Eric Arthur Simms, entered this world at two o'clock in the morning in an upstairs room of the Cottage which still stands at the north-east corner of Ladbroke Square in North Kensington in London. My mother was then thirty-seven years old and my father forty-eight.

My mother's father, Henry Coles, was the son of a former Oxford college servant and upholsterer. The Coleses were deeply rooted in Oxfordshire and it seems likely that some of my forbears had farmed in Blenheim Park. After being displaced from there they moved into Woodstock and Oxford to seek new employment. Henry Coles, who had married a book sewer, Ann Barnard, in 1875, lived in Clarendon Street. There were seven children of their union. My mother, Amy Margaret, was the fifth child, born on 25 May 1884. She married my father Levi Simms, on 25 December 1907 at the United Methodist Free Church in Oxford. My mother was a gentle devoted person, extremely active and conscientious, who made the upbringing of her four children her whole life. My father's tribute to her in a letter said everything: 'I know you realize as I do that she is a wife and mother in a thousand!'

My father's home was in Cheshire and many of his ancestors bear such typically Cheshire family names as Burgess, Hickson, Steele, Hassall, Baskerville and Brereton. Like all family trees his is varied and interesting, spanning the social scale and embracing both the essayist Sir Richard Steele and the other

Richard Steele who met his death in Barthomley Church at the hands of the King's men in October 1644. My great grandfather, John Burgess, lived in the Cheshire village of Odd Rode and his daughter Ann married my grandfather Thomas Simms. Their home was at Broughton Cottage in Rode Heath opposite the Broughton Arms, close to the Trent and Mersey Canal. It was here that my father was born on 19 November 1872 – the son, grandson and great-grandson of boatmen whose lives had been spent working on the canal which he could see as a boy from the windows of his house. It seemed very appropriate that the centenary year of my father's birth saw the transmission on BBC television of a film about Cheshire which I introduced standing by the canal with Broughton Cottage in the background.

My father kept a diary of recollections and impressions and one of his earliest memories was that of his grandmother, Lucy Burgess, 'walking up and down the newly ploughed fields picking stones. These were intended for repairing highways.' My father also wrote with affection of his own father who 'was, in his younger days, a boatman working boats to the canal's end at Runcorn. The cargoes were mostly salt blocks destined for shipment to vessels for South Africa and South America. He recalled a trip in a blizzard which killed his horse and gave him rheumatic fever. He was expert in making skeleton ships, full-rigged. The curved hull was made from thin wood split from the round side of cheese boxes. The ships were then dipped in the boiling salt brine, and they were frosted with a granular coating of dried salt.'

With the closure of the Lawton salt works and a rundown in the use of the canals, my father, on leaving school at the age of twelve, had to look elsewhere for employment. His first wages he drew as an errand boy and then in 1884 he went to work at Alsager Parsonage for six shillings a week with board. My father was then employed by a draper in Alsager in 1894, but two years later he decided, 'If horses mean livery, I'm leaving!' In spite of what my brother Wilfrid called this 'incipient rebelliousness' and perhaps because of it, he began to master the art of writing and speaking in public on horticultural, social and religious topics.

He was now drawn towards Oxford, where he felt that he might have a better chance of both employment and further education. He took lodgings in Plantation Road with my grandfather's sister, Mary Coles, and so began his association with the Coles family that was to lead to his meeting and eventually marrying my mother. On 30 January 1899 he entered Ruskin Hall as its third student but carried on with his job as foreman of Gee's horticultural nursery in the Banbury Road. In 1907 he married.

My eldest brother Thomas was born in 1908 in Oxford. Then my parents moved to London and Wilfrid was born three years later in Winchmore Hill. My father was appointed head gardener at Ladbroke Square and it was in the Cottage that my sister Margaret was born in 1914 and myself in 1921. I have many happy memories of this L-shaped house – a two-storeyed mid-Victorian dormer-windowed and ivy-covered cottage. Between 1849 and 1858 a row of large houses was built along the north side of Ladbroke Square, part of Thomas Allom's romantic concept of linked and stuccoed houses fitting into a wider scheme of terraces, road junctions and pleasing vistas which formed the Ladbroke Estate, laid out over the Hippodrome racecourse. At the eastern end of the row was a triangular space in which a head gardener's cottage was built. The front of the Cottage looked out over the square.

My father's main duties were to supervise the garden and two under-gardeners. I have actually held in my hands the original plan of the garden drawn up by Thomas Allom – an exercise in geometry with its paths laid out in large ovals and circles with curiously twisting and kidney-shaped flower-beds and most of the larger trees planted in groups of three. Each year, under my father's watchful eye, bloomed a succession of yellow and lavender Maximilian crocuses, daffodils and narcissi, iris, lupins, veronicas, geraniums and chrysanthemums, Hugh Dickson and Caroline Testout roses. The square was also quite rich in bird species.

It was in this delightful atmosphere of a *rus in urbe* that I grew up. I learned to look forward to the seasons and my interest in birds awoke at quite an early stage. At the age of three I apparently brought a young blue tit for my mother to see and returned it quite safely, saying that the parents had just fed it and would not be back for a few minutes. My mother created a warm and reassuring environment and I was able to see my father express his love for living things. I watched him match the tempo of his beloved garden, claiming that 'if a man is content with little he has the right to exert himself no more than is necessary to satisfy his simple wants'.

I first went to school at the age of six as my mother had undertaken my early instruction in the three R's to the apparent satisfaction of the school attendance officer. There were forty-two boys in my class in the gabled and red brick Portobello Road LCC School in North Kensington to which I was sent in the wake of my brothers and a distinguished Astronomer Royal, Sir Harold Spencer Jones. My class teacher was one of the many Welshmen who had come to teach in London schools after the First World War. I quite liked school and welcomed the social contacts. These were years of sooty coal fires, dusty playgrounds and the smell of onions frying in the backs of the tenements that overlooked the well-trodden asphalt.

The headmaster was a very forbidding figure with deeply lined face, frock-coat, striped trousers, winged collar and heavy gold watch-chain. Corporal punishment was regular in the school and I recall with horror the figure of a small terrified boy being forcibly held down across a chair and savagely flogged. I cannot remember his misdemeanour but I was made mortally afraid by that demonstration of official ruthlessness and used to wake up at night in a cold sweat. So perhaps for me it was a deterrent! Since then things have changed and later my sister Margaret was in fact, for some time a governor of the school.

But there were many compensations in my childhood. There was the wonderland of the Portobello Road market on a Saturday morning when one could see books, records, plates, clothes, even geological specimens all on sale at working-class prices. There were muffin men ringing their bells on a Sunday afternoon and the lamplighters going round as dusk fell. There was winter in Kensington – here recorded in one of my brother Thomas's poems published in 1932:

> The mist had settled, globular minute pearls,
> damping the blackened twigs; the sky's dull glow
> mingled with watery lamplight, paler yellow,
> and the pale fog in iridescent swirls.

There was the Round Pond in Kensington Gardens where I fished for sticklebacks and sailed an old pot-bellied yacht.

One day when I was very young I saw the sea at Southend but it was not until I was seven that its immensity and special magic were fully revealed to me. My parents took me to Brighton for the day and I paddled and splashed about under the chalk cliffs. Then we walked through Patcham, then undeveloped, over the Downs to Ditchling Beacon. Here under the great grassy scarp was a bungalow – the home of George Harwood – an old friend of my father. He had given up the routine of office life to become a freelance artist. An excellent botanist, a competent bird-watcher, a man with an enquiring mind, he was to have a great influence on my development as a naturalist. In 1932 I stayed for several weeks at his Sussex home from which I explored the great whale-backed hills for birds and the chalk quarries for my first Cretaceous fossils and prehistoric flint tools.

I was, of course, fortunate that my parents allowed me to indulge my early interest in natural history. I was reading avidly and some of my early presents included books by Charles G. D. Roberts, Richard Kearton and Henry Williamson. I bred guinea-pigs and learned about Mendelian inheritance. There were always animals about at home – two cats that I rescued from the square, a mongrel dog, Roman snails from the Downs, injured fledgling birds and tanks containing a motley assortment of great water beetles, water boatmen, leeches, and goldfish. Thomas became engaged to Mollie Payne, the daughter of two Baptist missionaries from China. She was very kind to me and gave me minnows and dace for my fish collection and once brought me a North American catfish in a dry paper bag. This horrific animal became my pride and joy and so tame that I could both handle it and feed it out of water.

In 1932 I won a Junior County Scholarship and in September

started at Latymer Upper School in Hammersmith, once again following in the path of my brothers. In my first term I found myself sitting next to another boy, Stanley Wood, the son of an official in the Inland Revenue, who lived in Shepherd's Bush. For the next seven years we were to share the same desk, specialize in the same subjects, indulge in friendly but keen academic rivalry, row in the School First Eight and develop a lifelong and valued friendship. I also made friends in Ladbroke Square with other children of my own age – John Gritten, son of the Conservative MP for Hartlepools, Alfred Nathan, with whom I played countless games of cricket, and Nicolette Bernard, the distinguished actress, for whom I developed an early distant passion.

I came to know a number of local residents who used the square for recreation and were subscribers to it. There was Miss Letitia Chitty who had worked on the stress problems of the R.100 and R.101 airships, designed dams and was later awarded the Telford Gold Medal – the highest award of the Institute of Civil Engineers. Her mother Mrs Mabel Chitty, was a great supporter of the Middlesex Cricket Club and took me on many days to Lord's where I could revel in the batting of Patsy Hendren, Wally Hammond, and Frank Woolley, and the bowling of Hedley Verity, Harold Larwood and Gubby Allen. Dr Rose Graham invited me to her home and gave me a copy of her treatise on the English monasteries, and Helena Hirst, wife of the economist Francis Hirst, presented me with a copy of H. A. L. Fisher's *A History of Europe*.

There were other interesting figures too who would stop and talk with a small boy watching the birds or doing his homework on a bench in the square – Sir Stephen Tallents, Sir Lawrence Bragg, Edmund Dulac and others. And, of course, there was the volatile figure of Sir William Davison, the Conservative MP for South Kensington for twenty-seven years, and later Lord Broughshane. He looked upon himself as my father's employer on behalf of the trustees of the square, but in practice he never quite achieved total success in this!

Colonel Richard Meinertzhagen – soldier, explorer and outspoken ornithologist – lived in Kensington Park Gardens. A high Tory of Danish descent he had been head of General

Allenby's Intelligence Section in 1916 and was responsible for the haversack ploy before the Third Battle of Gaza when he rode into the Turkish outposts. He was fired on, pretended to be wounded and dropped a haversack full of papers, money and letters, prepared for German Intelligence, and stained with fresh blood. These played a major part in deceiving the Turks as to the direction of Allenby's attack. He became the Chief Political Officer for Palestine and Syria after the war and then military adviser to Winston Churchill in the Colonial Office. One of the most colourful and remarkable officers the Army has ever had, he was described by Lawrence of Arabia as 'a silent, laughing masterful man, with an immensely powerful body and a savage brain'. A nephew of Beatrice Webb, he was one of Britain's most unconventional imperialists, a protagonist of Zionism, an almost legendary figure who saw the British Empire wither away under his eyes. He could only have lived in that remarkable era which has now passed away.

I often played with Colonel Meinertzhagen's three children whom I knew as Anne, Dan and Ran. He invited me to tea many times and sometimes we were joined by his cousin, Theresa Clay, the authority on bird parasites. He allowed me to inspect his collection of bird skins – a priceless ornithological treasure that eventually came to the nation. To an enthusiastic schoolboy naturalist like me he was kindness itself, sending round copies of *British Birds* and *The Ibis* and corresponding with me from all over the world. Whenever I had a problem about a bird he would always say 'Come round and have tea, and we'll talk about it.' It was quite an experience to have known this man whom General Smuts called mad and who, on meeting Adolf Hitler, had responded promptly to the greeting 'Heil Hitler!' with a sharp 'Heil Meinertzhagen!' Dan was lost in action in 1944 but his father lived until 1967, finally departing from a world he said 'I shall not be sorry to leave.'

Latymer Upper School, founded in 1624, was a solid-style school off King Street in Hammersmith with a sound record of scholarships at Oxford and Cambridge. Thomas had left in 1926 to go to Merton and from there to a post at Lawrence Sheriff School in Rugby. Wilfrid, after following him to Oxford and Merton, became a master at Sherborne where bird photographer George Yeates was also on the staff. Margaret was attending the Godolphin and Latymer School not far away. For me the first five years at the new school were a steady drive towards my school certificate examinations. I was petrified by the Latin master who demonstrated '*ad* with the accusative' – 'Motion, boy!' – by throwing blackboard rubbers at the windows. I had considerable difficulty with chemistry, despite the master's attempts to set us analysing unknown salts to the lilt of:

>Am. sulphide to basic liq.
>Brings down Zinc, Man, Co and Nick.

I was enthralled by my history master, L. G. Brandon, who brought a new and inward glow to facts and dates and it is perhaps especially to him that I owe any ability I have to look backwards and recreate the scenes and events of past eras. I also remember with affection Graham 'Bunter' Sutton, the father of Shaun Sutton, Head of BBC Television Drama. Novelist, playwright, lecturer and mountaineer, he was one of Latymer's best-loved figures. We boys could always persuade him to leave the boring topic of a set lesson to demonstrate vividly on a classroom window-sill how he had climbed Great Gable.

Life in the middle school was full of action. I boxed and played football for the school, as my general health improved with puberty. At lunchtime I used to slip off to the grounds of nearby Chiswick House to watch jays, great spotted woodpeckers and kingfishers at close range. By this time I was reading the Waverley novels, Dickens, H. G. Wells, H. M. Tomlinson and I found an adolescent solace in the introspective rather self-pitying poetry of Swinburne and the novels of Henry Williamson. I also began to write for the school magazine – romances and poems. In 1936 Wilfrid gave me an 1833 edition of Gilbert White's *Natural History of Selborne* which was to prove a shining beacon for the rest of my life as a naturalist. I was now beginning to list and study the birds in Ladbroke Square in great detail and soon I had turned my attention to the Royal Parks as well. Then there was Holland Park. This great open space in West London belonged to the Earl of Ilchester and was opened to the public on a Saturday in May at the cost of a shilling entrance fee for those who wished to enjoy the rose garden. Photography was my father's favourite hobby and, while he was taking studies of the House, I was off to the secluded northern half of the woodlands in search of birds which I had heard or glimpsed as I exercised our dog Teddy along Holland Walk. Fool's parsley and bluebells grew under the canopy of the trees and the bird choruses were of great power and variety. Here I found jays, green and great spotted woodpeckers, stock doves, tawny owls, marsh tits and in 1937 I discovered a chiffchaff's nest – the first recorded nest in Inner London.

By this time I had acquired a second-hand cycle which enabled me to reach birdy areas farther afield. I often cycled across London to Selsdon in Surrey to carry out dawn-chorus watches and then I went to my Aunt Ethel's house for a very welcome breakfast. I discovered Beddington Sewage Farm with its reed and sedge warblers and, since George Harwood had left Sussex to live in Welwyn Garden City, I turned north into Hertfordshire for nightingales, corncrakes and cirl buntings. When I was just sixteen he wrote to me: 'Have you ever thought of going in for any original research into bird matters yourself? You must have done enough passive observing and accumulated an enormous quantity of data by now. Why not strike out a new path, set yourself some specific bird problem and concentrate all your time and energy in solving it?' I hope that as he botanizes and paints in the Elysian Fields he can nod his head with some satisfaction at what this advice eventually achieved.

In 1937 I cycled over to Richmond Park and there for the first time I met C. L. Collenette. A tall, sparse figure of a man, he had carried out research into the moths of French Guinea, the Pacific, East Africa and the Mato Grosso. He was an excellent botanist and bird-watcher and I found him a good friend and counsellor. He personally introduced me to the London Natural History Society whose members at that time included Richard Fitter, P. A. D. (Phil) Hollom, E. R. (John) Parrinder, Dr Geoffrey Beven, E. M. (Max) Nicholson and, of course, Arthur Holte Macpherson who lived not far away on Campden Hill and entered into a regular correspondence with me.

Also in 1937 Dr E. Dale retired from the headmastership of Latymer. He was succeeded by F. W. Wilkinson who had taught under Sanderson of Oundle and who came from the headship of the Polytechnic School in Regent's Street. With a less remote figure at the helm a new regime was introduced to the school. He started a boat club and coffee evenings for his sixth-formers. I was lucky enough to join Stanley Wood in the First Eight and I rowed between him and the stroke, W. I. Percival, who went on to become an MP, QC and a Recorder. I was invited to watch the Oxford and Cambridge Boat Race from the roof of Naomi Mitchison's house on Hammersmith Mall. Professor J. B. S. Haldane's sister had written many attractive historical books which I had enjoyed and I remember how my visit that day was crowned by a notable Oxford rowing success.

It was quite clear in the 1930s that there was no chance of my becoming a professional ornithologist and so with a well-established interest in history it was natural that, like my brothers, I should enter the History Sixth Form. Here I came under the influence of A. D. Sopwith, the senior history master. A Tynesider and a bachelor, he was devoted to teaching. Logical and meticulous in manner, he awakened in us a proper scepticism. My two years in the Sixth coincided with momentous events in Europe. I was certain that war was coming, following the betrayal of Spain, the destruction of Ethiopia and the German annexation of Austria and Czechoslovakia.

My adolescence proceeded fairly calmly, due probably to the old pedagogic precepts of 'Work hard, play hard!' I was clearly heterosexual but had not yet kissed a girl and only admired or coveted them from afar. I was becoming interested in plays and became a fairly regular visitor to the Old Vic. I was learning to appreciate classical music and regularly attended the promenade concerts at the old Queen's Hall. After getting to know the dancer Prudence Hyman and her sister Cherry, I became quite a balletomane, cycling out to Sadlers Wells or dropping into the Mercury Theatre at Notting Hill Gate to see the Ballet Rambert. Film-going came late in my life.

The first film that I saw was Herbert Ponting's study of Antarctic penguins at the Kensington Cinema and the second was John Grierson's *Drifters*. I watched many educational films at the Imperial Institute on Saturday mornings but real cinema did not begin for me before the Sixth Form.

I was fortunate enough to be offered a Board of Education Grant to go to Merton and also to be awarded a King's Scholarship at the University of London. There was no hesitation in my mind which I would accept. The next hurdle was Higher Schools Certificate. Then there was nothing to do for the remainder of the term. Freed from the anxieties of work, we rowed in many regattas and piloted our Eight *Felix* through countless locks above Richmond to Staines Regatta. I was invited by Alan Thomas, the editor of *The Listener*, to represent the view of the secondary schoolboy in a symposium on education. For the first time I entered the portals of Broadcasting House, unaware that just over a decade later I would have my own office on the fifth floor!

Later in August my father took me for a few days to visit his brother Harold in Stoke-on-Trent and to tour the countryside of his boyhood. The international situation was getting worse and on top of that my father and I arrived back in London in the face of a threatened rail strike. It was my eighteenth birthday. School reopened on the 25th and within three days the masters and boys of Latymer were ready to leave London at a moment's notice. On 31 August the signal was received and on the following day the school left for 'an unknown destination'. In the event this turned out to be Windsor station from which the party split into five groups and was dispersed to Gerrards Cross, Richings Park, Horton, Farnham Common and Iver Heath. I was billeted in Iver Heath and here it was that I heard both Chamberlain's declaration of war over the radio and the air-raid alarm that quickly followed it. There was little more that I could do, so I said goodbye to the girl in the village shop and went home to await developments. And eventually the message came that the university at Oxford was going to open after all and would I come up to Merton on Friday, 13 October.

3

Oxford in Wartime

We had stopped, as trains would on many later occasions, outside the cemetery just short of Oxford station. Behind me and beyond the Hinksey Stream was the square tower of South Hinksey church and the graveyard where my mother's parents lay at rest. To the right was the flinty block of Oxford Castle and beyond that the spires of the city. I pondered on the prospect of life ahead of me – it was still a wonder that the university was opening at all. In September 1939 a plan had been devised between the university and the Ministry of Works whereby some colleges, like Brasenose, would be totally requisitioned, some including Merton taken over only in part, while others such as University College would be reserved as reception colleges to take men from the commandeered colleges as well as their own undergraduates.

Merton was already to some extent familiar to me. Founded in 1264 by Walter de Merton, Chancellor to Henry III, the college is graced by a number of fine buildings and a pleasant walled garden. There is no more moving experience than to see the pinnacles of the great Merton tower soaring up from Mob Quad into the rose-glow of dawn or shining silver-grey in the light of a full moon. In 1939 the Ministry of Works requisitioned the whole of Grove and 'Stubbins' Buildings as well as part of Front Quad and Fellows Quad. As a result I and fifty other Merton freshmen were banished to University College while Merton filled up with typists, secretaries, and marching WAAFs, and also housed the Ministry of Aircraft Production and the planning centre of a vast organization for repairing crashed aircraft which made a significant contribution to Allied air supremacy.

In 'Univ', as University College was called, I shared a study with Alex Wheater, a blunt Yorkshireman from Coatham School who had come up in 1938 to read English under Edmund Blunden. He later became a schoolmaster. Our room on the first floor overlooked the High Street and the florid finials and honey-coloured stone slates of All Souls' roof. In one direction I could follow the traffic flowing beyond St Mary's towards Carfax. In the other I could see the front of Queen's and Longwall Street where Lord Nuffield, as a young man, had repaired my father's bicycle with his own hands.

My tutor was Idris Deane Jones who had become a Fellow of Merton in 1921 and had also known Thomas and Wilfrid. He was now Senior Tutor and a stimulating and gifted teacher who had brought a great deal of inspiration to all his students. His wife Muriel had a keen sense of humour and a marvellous ability to put new undergraduates at ease. Among the freshmen were John Campsie, who later went into publishing, Arthur Jacobs the music critic and author, M. C. Thursby-Pelham, who rowed with me and went on to become Commandant of the Guards' Depot, Hugh Smith and Philip Stibbe, both schoolmasters, and Douglas Grant, who became a distinguished soldier and Professor of American Literature at Leeds University. These I knew well and I also became very friendly with two more senior scholars – Frank Bonsall from Bishop's Stortford College and Donald Rawcliffe from Wallasey Grammar School – and the three of us used to explore the Oxfordshire countryside together.

The first term, marked by the 'phoney war', was a curiously suspended time in which the uncertainty made life difficult and yet in many ways Oxford went on as if nothing were amiss. I survived the initiation of the Freshers' Blind, began to find out how the university worked, rowed and investigated the societies and clubs. I was introduced to the sheer delight of concerts held on Sundays in the hall of Balliol.

And in this new and stimulating atmosphere there was also ornithology. I joined the Oxford Ornithological Society. At this time the president was Bernard Tucker, and the secretary, N. A. Watson from New College, fired me with enthusiasm to help with the bird-ringing trap in Christchurch Meadows, just at the back of Merton. I also went to see W. B. Alexander, the author of that original field guide *The Birds of the Ocean* and the Director of the Edward Grey Institute which was then based at 39 Museum Road. From that first visit stemmed a whole series of ornithological outings in which W. B. took me in his car to count the pochard, pintail and grebes at Cassington gravel pits or further afield to south Warwickshire and the Berkshire Downs. For a budding ornithologist these were valuable days in the country.

Frank Bonsall, Donald Rawcliffe and I managed to cycle out on a number of days to Otmoor – an area of fenny desolation 'cast under a spell of ancient magic' which lies about six miles to the north-east of Oxford. In the embrace of such delightful villages as Charlton-on-Otmoor, Wood Eaton, Oddington and Noke, this strange bit of country became a favourite resort of mine outside Oxford. There was an RAF bombing range on Otmoor – I came to use it a few years later – and it was not always possible to get right round. It was a fine spot for birds and Frank, Donald and I often saw wigeon and teal and more occasionally short-eared owls and merlins in winter, while the summer pleasures included redstarts, little owls and hobbies.

We worked hard and we played hard and there were other pleasing activities as well. There were regular invitations from Sir William, later Lord Beveridge, the Master of University College, to his At Homes. At these he and Mrs Jessy Mair, who had been his secretary at the Ministry of Munitions and later the London School of Economics, quickly put his guests at ease. I discussed with the craggy-faced Master many of the pressing issues of the time, including social insurance and those ideas of his that were to be crystallized in the Beveridge Plan which was to be published in December 1942. He was undoubtedly a man of passion, scholarly but perhaps a little artless.

There were pleasant evenings with Idris and Muriel Deane Jones and through them I met Leslie Banks – the stage and film actor – who lived in cobbled Merton Street where I became a frequent guest, playing exciting and endless games of table tennis with his two delightful daughters. There were occasional summonses to the Warden's Lodgings for coffee with Sir John Miles. And Professor H. W. Garrod would send me notes which might read: 'Dear Simms, Please come and help me entertain a pretty WAAF to tea today!' He was a Fellow of Merton and had been Professor of Poetry from 1923 to 1928. His whole life was the craft and study of poetry and he had written critical studies of Byron, Keats, Wordsworth and Coleridge. He once said: 'I think poorly of my scholarship but not too badly of my journalism.' Although a bit of a recluse, he liked young people and his courtesy and benevolence endeared him to generations of undergraduates who soon learned to recognize his spaniel and his battered hat. And I was always welcome to Sunday lunch in Polstead Road where my mother's elder sister Dora and my uncle Frank Fox lived while running the family business of the Kemp Hall Press.

The summer term in 1940 started under the shadow of the German blitzkrieg. I went back for the Hilary Term on 18 April – the same day that General Sir Bernard Paget landed at Andalsnes in central Norway in an attempt to recapture Trondheim, nine days after Denmark and Norway had been invaded by the Germans. For me there was an air of unreality about the university. For relief I cycled out to Iffley to look for fritillaries flowering in 'the grassy harvest of the river fields'. This was a brief interlude for me, but the term went on much as usual. Then the invasion of Holland, Belgium and Luxembourg on 10 May changed all that. As the news from France grew steadily worse men began to lose their orientation and their purpose. A classical scholar said to me, 'What the hell's the use of bothering with Latin and Greek when the modern world is turning upside down?' Emulating Seneca, several undergraduates opened their veins in baths and nervous breakdowns began to increase.

Unbelievably in retrospect Eights Week was still on and one day I took an early lunch in University College Dining Hall so that the joint Merton–University First Eight, by eating early, would be able to row a full practice course on the river at a time when it would be reasonably clear of punts and pleasure craft. I walked out alone across Front Quad, collected my cycle and went off down the High to reach the University College barge which rode proudly at anchor off the Meadows.

Oxford in Wartime

We rowed our course without incident and I returned to college only to find that it was out of bounds. When, after a long delay, I was allowed in, I saw a body lying under a tarpaulin just outside the entrance to the Dining Hall. Gradually I pieced together what had happened. An undergraduate with whom I had fortunately had amicable if not close relations had taken a service rifle and stationed himself by a window on a landing in the Porter's Lodge. From here, with his rifle resting on a pile of sandbags, he could hold in his sights everyone who left the Hall to cross the Quad. I must have left the Hall and walked along the path towards the Lodge with the rifle pointing right at me, since only a few seconds after I had entered the High, our disturbed marksman shot dead the first man to emerge from the Hall doorway. He was a crack shot and seriously wounded the next man, while a third, who had started to run on hearing the noise was struck in the leg by another shot. He left the rifle, went downstairs and was held as he was about to leave the Lodge.

Eights Week went ahead as if nothing unusual was happening although two days before the Germans had reached Abbeville and the English Channel. As the sandwich boat at the top of Division II we had to row the course twice each day. There were few people on the towpath but the racing was keen and we finally succeeded in bumping Corpus–Pembroke and St Peter's Hall, who were in front of us at the bottom of Division I. To celebrate we swam across the Isis and had tea on the barge.

On 22 June, France accepted Hitler's terms. On the following day I set off to cycle from Kensington through the city – at that time a not too difficult thing to do – along the Mile End Road to Brentwood, Chelmsford, Braintree and the rolling Suffolk countryside. Several times a Bren-gun carrier caught me up and soldiers wanted to know where I was going, while policemen at village crossroads, now devoid of signposts, put up warning hands to bring me to a halt. The long vacation was ahead and I intended to work for a couple of months on a Suffolk farm, recovering from the Dunkirk term and doing something that I thought was positively useful. The farm stood on a ridge where Neolithic flint knappers had once shaped their knives and arrowheads and where the plough was continually bringing Roman tiles and pots to the surface. Braggons lay between the villages of Glemsford and Boxted. Once farmed by an artist of considerable skill, F. E. Russell, who had ten years or so before invited Thomas to stay, it was now run by his daughter Monica and her husband. As I worked in the cornfields there was a chain of skylark song overhead and the harsh shacking calls of red-legged partridges all round me. From the great field by Glemsford Church drifted the faint rattle of a binder at work and from the west came the sharp chatter of a machine-gun as England prepared her defences against the foreign invader. The summer of 1940 passed and the harvest was brought in. At the end of August, with two paintings by Russell, a chicken and a bag of flint knives and other artifacts strapped to my cycle, I set off for London.

At the Cottage life was reassuringly normal. But on the late afternoon of 7 September 300 German bombers with an escort of 600 fighters attacked London in two separate raids. I watched the bombers flying over Central London and bombs began to rain down on the London docks and the tiny streets of the East End. From Ladbroke Square it was soon possible to see a giant black cloud of smoke rising thousands of feet above the city. As the evening sky began to darken, the cloud changed to rose and then a fiery red. The blazing docks and streets brought attack by night and bombs went on cascading into the inferno until nearly five o'clock the next morning. Hermann Goering then issued orders for the area covered by the German attacks to be enlarged. The nights now took on a regular and soon a very familiar plan. First came the sirens in the evening, then the 'poom-poom' of the anti-aircraft guns in Hyde Park, the beat of unsynchronized bomber engines overhead and then the bangs of the battery on Wormwood Scrubs. We sheltered under the kitchen table and under the great solid wooden dresser bolted to the wall. Night after night there were the rush and sickening thud of bursting bombs, the whine and metallic ring of shrapnel and the nose cones of shells falling in the streets, the stench of charred rubble. My father's deafness saved him a great deal of worry during these trying days. One night six incendiaries fell on the Cottage walls but not through the roof. I have the base of one of them on my desk and it bears the date 1936.

As October went on, the Battle of Britain began to peter out, but my father gave up his job at Ladbroke Square after twenty-nine years and he and my mother left Inner London for good. I was now living in Merton itself and the modern conditions and facilities in the new buildings in Rose Lane compared very favourably with the somewhat spartan life in 'Univ'. Edmund Blunden was the College fire officer and it seemed strange that this distinguished soldier who served in France and Belgium between 1916 and 1919 was organizing the college's air-raid precautions. Oxford itself escaped attack from the air. I joined the Oxford University Air Squadron and was given a deferment until the end of the academic year – June 1941. Initial training in the squadron took up a lot of time and I was also busy serving as the steward of the Junior Common Room with the Rugby blue R. W. Pennock as president.

Early in 1941 my parents moved north to the ancient and delightful town of Appleby in Westmorland. Set in the valley of the River Eden, it was then the county town. My father was going to look after the gardens of Castle Bank – a pink, bow-windowed house below the castle which belonged to the composer and musician Lady Holmes, the widow of a former Director of the National Gallery. At the end of term I travelled up to Westmorland for the first time. The journey by train took me through a strange high land of moors and fells and I shall never forget this first impact that mountains made on me. From the windows of the coach I looked out in awe on these ice-smoothed blocks of stone, eroded and bare near their misty, snowy summits and streaked with lines of greyish scree and drifts of dead brown bracken. This was a new and vastly appealing world that stirred the romantic in me. From that first glimpse arose my lifelong love and need for mountain landscapes to contemplate and high fells to set my feet upon.

Castle Bank was built below Caesar's Tower, as the keep was known – a fortress once held by Lady Anne Clifford for Charles I. The house stood by the River Eden, facing Bongate Mill and the long diagonal weir where the salmon used to leap. My parents' home was a low grey stone bungalow above the house and with long views towards the fells. The morning after my arrival was one of those rare warm northern spring days and my mother and I wandered along the banks of the Eden through the grassy watermeadows and tangy pinewoods, talking together and pausing to watch the curlews feeding in the fields. We idled our way as far as Great Ormside on that lovely morning and along the horizon ran the fells like the grey backbone of some vast dead dinosaur.

One of our favourite walks was through Flakebridge Woods, which were full of bird songs, and up into the deep and ominous cleft in the Pennines called High Cup Nick; here the great band of igneous rock known as the Whin Sill shows itself after running under northern England all the way from the Farne Islands. I delighted in following the becks and their courses deep into the massif of carboniferous limestone hills. There were several pairs of dippers on Hilton Beck and curlews and lapwings on the slopes of the fells. I climbed up Mell Fell, Murton Pike and Roman Fell, getting to know the terrain in anticipation of longer expeditions across the spine of England. I traversed the great snow-beds on Hilton Fell where red grouse and even twite could be heard calling. From the barytes mines high up Hilton Beck I was able to fill my pockets with clear and topaz-coloured crystals of quartz, fluorspar and calcite. At Scordale Mine galena was worked as long ago as the fourteenth century.

I followed the Maize Beck up to the River Tees and Caldron Snout. On these high bare summits I really learned for the first time what true solitude can mean. This land of farmsteads and hillside villages, of pastures and grey stone walls, of fells and rocky spurs, of crags and boulders, was one that I came to love and respect.

The summer of 1941 saw the approach of my final examinations. On 22 June the Germans attacked Russia and it looked as if we in Britain had been granted a respite. After the examinations, which took place in a heat-wave, were over and term had ended – my last as an undergraduate – I returned to Appleby. Here I explored my beloved fells and the mountains above the Cumberland lakes. It was in these surroundings that I spent my last weeks awaiting my call-up into the RAF.

4

Call-Up

The waiting was over! A long buff envelope dropped on to the front doormat at Castle Bank. I was instructed to report to the Aircrew Reception Centre at Regent's Park on 16 August. At four o'clock on a summery day I assembled with a group of other civilians in Baker Street. Among them was an old friend, Denys Street, who had been with me in the Oxford University Air Squadron. A smart RAF flight sergeant soon had us shuffling off along Prince Albert Road in search of our quarters. These were large blocks of commandeered flats – Stafford Court, Bentinck Close, Avenue Close – which lay to the north of Regent's Park. In the early morning we could be seen marching in flights along the Outer Circle of the nearby park and towards the zoo where one of the restaurants served as the airmen's mess. As we lined up in solid blocks of men along the roadway we could hear the maniacal laughter of gibbons in their outdoor cages, the ironic barks of sea-lions in their pool and the scream of macaws in the parrot house.

One day we all marched round to a garage near St John's Wood Church to be kitted out with uniform from ill-fitting greatcoat to tie, with webbing equipment, hold-alls, housewife, forage cap and boots. The last item was entirely functional and Denys Street, requiring size 14s, had to remain behind, after we had been posted, for a pair to be specially prepared. I never saw him again. Denys, who was the son of Sir Arthur Street, the Permanent Under-Secretary for Air, was murdered in cold blood by the Germans, together with forty-nine other officers, after the mass escape from Stalag Luft III. We had PT on Lord's cricket ground and signals training in the Pavilion.

Lectures were given in a local cinema on the RAF, admin., and VD.

Exactly four weeks after I had been posted to Regent's Park, we were on our way by train to Torquay where I was to spend a fairly undemanding six months at No. 3 Initial Training Wing (ITW). I lived in a commandeered hotel, the Regina, which overlooked the harbour and the waters of Torbay. Our CO was Squadron Leader J.J.F. Pennink, the former British amateur golf champion. We did a lot of square-bashing on the front under a rugged ramrod, Sergeant Board, and became rather proud of our drill technique. We carried out navigation exercises in launches on Torbay among the gannets, auks and fulmars. There were sea cliffs and the picturesque villages of the hinterland to explore. It was a pleasant autumn in Torquay and the sea was delightful to swim in.

I spent a great deal of time pounding the pavements outside the Regina Hotel on guard duty, saluting wing commanders and squadron leaders many of whom were really flying officers and flight lieutenants with acting ranks. One day an Arctic skua flew low past my guard post in hot pursuit of a terrified herring gull and on another occasion a peregrine falcon plucked a small bird on the pavement outside the hotel.

Way back in 1936 the Air Ministry had looked at the possibility of an Empire Air Training Scheme whereby aircrew could be trained overseas. By 1942 the idea had become a reality and an organization was set up capable of producing 11 000 pilots and 17 000 other aircrew every year. There were training facilities in Canada, South Africa and Rhodesia, while under the Arnold Plan arrangements were also made to train pilots in the United States. I opted for Canada or Africa but found myself bound for the States.

But I was first sent to No. 21 Elementary Flying Training School at Booker, near Marlow, in Buckinghamshire. Here I joined up with Alan Skempton, who later became a BBC news reader, and Derek Boyden, who was to open up the American market for Schweppes after the war. Booker was equipped with DH 82as – Tiger Moths – those fine trainer biplanes which entered service with the RAF in 1932 and were one of the most famous and well-liked aeroplanes ever to be designed. My instructor Pilot Officer H. Kelsey, introduced me to the sensation of flying. I have a curious recollection of receding and advancing ground, of toy houses and roads, of my views of the clouds in a blue sky spinning round and being replaced by others of dingy earth and green fields all rotating past my eyes as if superimposed on a giant disk.

After ten hours of flying in the same machine, T 6815, I was given a check flight by Squadron Leader Kelsey, my instructor's brother, which I passed. Now I knew that the moment of truth was at hand! I was going to have to fly this machine solo. And on 29 March after half an hour's demonstrations and practice of take-offs and landings with Pilot Officer Kelsey we taxied to a halt. The palms of my hands began to sweat and there was a pink flush of apprehension on my cheeks. Was he about to abandon me or not? He talked to me for a few minutes in the aircraft, underlining the basic points of circuits and bumps. Then suddenly without warning he levered himself up in the front cockpit and clambered out of the aircraft.

'Right! It's all yours! Make a good job of it!'

As soon as my instructor was clear I began to taxi the Tiger Moth forward, swinging her slightly from side to side so that I could see ahead of me. I glanced at the windsock and turned into the slight breeze blowing across the airfield. I looked all round me, above and behind – it was clear! I slowly but firmly pushed the throttle lever forward and the Tiger Moth began to bump along the grass. As we gathered speed I gently eased the stick forward, the tail lifted and, under the power of her Gipsy engine, she rose up like a bird. Soon I had to make the decision to turn to the left – to port. I looked at the airfield away to my left and saw some tiny figures and a Tiger Moth landing on the grass. Now for the real decision! I have to judge the critical moment when to cut the engine for a gliding approach and effect my last left-hand turn to line up for the actual landing. The roar of the engine stops and I begin a quiet, fluttering descent towards the grass. The wind sighs and strains through the wires between the wings.

'Steady now! Keep her level!' I call out, encouraging myself for the crisis immediately ahead. The aircraft is now floating a few feet above the green field. 'Very steady! Ease the stick back!'

The speed is falling off. Bang! The Tiger Moth hits the ground simultaneously on all three wheels. I have managed a three-point landing and I am down in one piece.

Pilot Officer Kelsey says, 'Take her up for half an hour and don't get lost!'

And so I fly T 6815 up over the houses once more and find the railway line from High Wycombe to Princes Risborough. It is a glorious spring afternoon and the air is very clear. I turn west to Thame and Wheatley and make a run to Oxford. Soon I can see a straggle of tiny houses and then a fan of streets stretching away from the Plain. There is Magdalen Bridge and tree-fringed Christchurch Meadows. I can look down on the college barges lying like driftwood on the Isis, on the Kemp Hall Press and the great stone square of Tom Quad. I can also pick out Merton Chapel and the Radcliffe Camera, standing isolated like a chess piece.

After being assessed as 'making satisfactory progress' as a pilot, I went to Appleby for my embarkation leave. Spring had come to Castle Bank but the ash trees still stood bare in winter garb. The first willow warbler had returned and song thrushes were nesting in the beech hedge.

I was eventually summoned to Heaton Park near Prestwich to the north of Manchester. On reporting I received several inoculatory jabs in the arm and was handed a piece of paper on which was scrawled an address.

'That's your billet!' bawled the sergeant.

'But where is it?' I enquired.

'Next!' shouted the NCO.

Clutching the bit of paper in one hand and staggering under the weight of three kitbags – I had full flying gear with me – I set off on my mission. It was raining hard now as I made my way through lines of undistinguished terraced houses. My punctured arm began to swell. My greatcoat was soaking up the rain like a sponge and I was feeling pretty low. A door in one of these houses opened.

'Coom on, luv! You coom inside!'

'But I'm soaking wet!'

'Never thee mind!' was the kindly response, and I found myself standing on some green linoleum in a tidy polished hall

Call-Up

with rivulets of water trickling down from my coat. A stout motherly woman in her fifties, full of concern and compassion, she soon brewed me a life-saving cup of tea and explained where my billet was. Only half a mile to go!

On 28 April our Arnold draft boarded a train on the first part of our journey to the United States. It threaded its way through the familiar towns for me of Skipton and Settle and then stopped, tantalizingly enough, in Appleby station for at least half an hour. We reached Gourock on the Clyde and transferred to lighters. We pulled alongside a 15 000-ton transport called HMTS *Banfora* and clambered aboard. More than 3000 airmen crowded on to this ship, taking over deck space and table-tops as sleeping quarters. I found a hammock – there were precious few of these – and a place to sling it above; it was across a companionway from which I could reach the open deck in five seconds flat! If we were torpedoed I wanted to die in the open sea, not among a panic-stricken mob of men below decks. We sailed at 6.15 pm on the 29th in the company of a large freighter adorned with big yellow derricks. As escort we had four lend-lease destroyers, each sporting four upright funnels. As we steamed slowly past Bute, little parties of kittiwakes and razorbills flew across our bows. By the next day we were west of the Mull of Kintyre and I began to see Manx shearwaters and storm petrels. At this point the herring gulls that had left the Clyde with us decided to turn back.

The overcrowding of the troopship was serious. As the *Banfora* began to meet the Atlantic rollers, the decks and lavatories soon began to fill with grey hunched-up anonymous figures, aswill in vomit and with a look of utter despair on their faces. The food was dreadful and there were few to eat it. To avoid the unpleasantness below, I spent all the daylight hours on deck, watching the sea and the birds.

On 2 May I saw four pomarine skuas and a single great skua. The next day there were thirteen little auks and a Leach's petrel. At 55°N.27°30'W. six great shearwaters stationed themselves at the stern of the ship, gliding and banking on stiff, outstretched wings. A snow bunting, 575 miles from the nearest land, dropped in for a half hour's rest. On 4 May I spotted three sooty shearwaters and several Wilson's petrels.

On the ninth a few herring gulls came out to meet the ship and I knew that the voyage would soon be over. It had taken us ten days. In the afternoon we saw ahead of us the low coast-line of Nova Scotia and the *Banfora* slowly made her way up to Halifax.

We disembarked the next day and were shepherded on to a train that took us through woodlands and apple orchards and stations bearing familiar names like Truro and Oxford or strange ones like Shubenacadie and Stewiacke. We were on our way to No. 31 PD at Moncton in New Brunswick where all RAF personnel entering and leaving the New World had to be processed. Derek Boyden and I billeted together in one of the white wooden huts and I met an old Merton friend, John Campsie. The following day was sunny and crisp and I explored Moncton itself – a typically open town with wooden houses and front steps, gardens without hedges, and a park, where I saw my first rusty blackbird, wood thrush and song sparrow. On a small lawn in front of a house was an American robin, newly arrived from the south and handsome with his grey back and rust-red breast. I bought a pound of bananas and solemnly ate them in the street – the first that I had tasted for two and a half years.

In front of us lay a five-day journey by train south to Albany in Georgia. Our troop train, which was equipped with couchettes, was pulled at the start by a giant Canadian Pacific locomotive, with bell and royal crown, which had hauled the train carrying King George VI and Queen Elizabeth across the Dominion. We steamed across New Brunswick and through the seemingly endless and birdless pine stands of Maine. From the orchards of the Lakes Peninsula we re-entered the United States through the corn belt of Ohio and the meat-packing city of Cincinnati. As we crossed the Tennessee River near Knoxville I was thrilled to see a rear-paddle steamer pushing steadily forward with clouds of dark smoke pouring out from its twin funnels. Eventually the longest train journey that I have ever undertaken brought us through Chattanooga, Atlanta and Macon into the cotton lands of the South and the town of Albany.

We were being posted to the United States Army Air

Force's Turner Field near Albany so that we could become acclimatized to the extreme heat and bright sun of the Deep South before starting our flying training. We lived in square wooden huts surrounded by gravel and with mosquito netting in the window-frames. The huts had pyramid-shaped tent-style roofs whose bottoms could be unrolled down the side frames to keep out rain and dust during the tremendous storms which afflicted Georgia. Iron beds were fitted inside and these had to be made down with forty-five-degree tucks at the base – fit enough to be measured by protractor. We were woken early in the morning by a very loud military brass band, complete with glockenspiel, which marched round the huts playing 'You gotta get up! You gotta get up! You gotta get up in the morning!'

There was barely time to wash and dress in our khaki tropical kit before having to fall in outside. We were also introduced to the life style of the USAAF. It was explained to disbelieving RAF cadets that the 'honour' system prevailed and so any airman spotting an infringement, however trivial, of the multitude of regulations must regard it as his duty to report it at once to an officer. There were black marks, known as demerits, for offences and for each one awarded above five there was an hour's marching at attention around the barrack square in off-duty time. Inspecting officers wearing white silk gloves would come and draw their fingers carefully over the tops of doors, over ledges, bed rails and so on. In Georgia the air was very dusty and it often blew hard, so that it was impossible not to collect demerits.

It is a strange and interesting fact that a number of colloquial and apparently harmless phrases in English take on totally different and highly significant meanings in the States. We were briefed about these but not about a certain emotive song. Because of this omission one party of well-intentioned but historically uninformed cadets lustily sang 'Marching through Georgia' to the consternation of the inhabitants of Albany!

5

Flame Vines and Spanish Moss

The great steam locomotive finally started to pull out from Albany. There was some subdued chatter in the coach, an occasional strident laugh, but my face was glued to the window. It was now 4 July. I had not flown since 29 March and I was getting restive. The news from home was rather worrying too – Rommel had stormed Tobruk and invaded Egypt, and Sebastopol had fallen. We had all read in awestruck silence about the 1000-bomber raid on Cologne, but here in this land of sun, peaches and fried chicken it was difficult to realize that a war was going on across the Atlantic.

In southern Georgia the townships were decked in roses – there were roses everywhere. From the train we looked out on bent figures in a sharp contrast of black skin and white shirts working in the brick-red fields or wandering among the swaying cottonheads. Here and there I caught a brief glimpse of the restful white of stately Georgian mansions at the end of long cool avenues of hickory trees. We were now moving steadily into the Deep South with its stands of long-leaved pines and live-oaks festooned with long strands of Spanish moss. We cleared the edge of the great Okefenokee Swamp and entered Jacksonville on the St John's River.

At this point I began to revel in my good fortune. My service life had brought me, at no expense to myself, to this mysterious region where childhood imagination and memories of far-off partly forgotten things had mixed up marvellous flowers, orange groves, alligators, egrets and Spaniards into a glorious amalgam of warmth, scent and colour. At last the train ran slowly into the station at Lakeland and the journey to Florida was over. Life for the next two months was to be organized almost entirely by the USAAF. We were to be given primary flying training at the civilian Lodwick School of Aeronautics just outside Lakeland.

Our group of cadets formed Class 43 A, while, just before our arrival, Class 42 J had departed for basic training elsewhere. This left the middle course – 42K – who still had four weeks of their eight-week course to go as the senior course, or, in American parlance, the 'Upperclass'. In theory this seniority granted Upperclassmen the right to 'haze' their juniors – the 'Lowerclassmen' – by giving them orders, however trivial, absurd or degrading, and expecting them to be carried out. It was the belief that this might be tough on you for four weeks, but, after all, be patient! In a month you would have progressed to Upperclass status yourself and you would be empowered to put the newcomers through the same delightful procedures. The honour system and the awarding of demerit marks that we had first encountered at Turner Field became very familiar.

We were made to march at the double all over the camp, even the few yards which separated the lecture rooms from the canteen, and the shouts of 'Hep, Tew, Three, Four!' reverberated around the barrack blocks. Inside the canteen Square Meals were the order of the day and this did not mean large helpings! This, to me quite incomprehensible, military custom, which as I saw in a recent television documentary still persists at Air Force and military academies in the States, consists of impaling a morsel of food with a fork, raising it parallel to the edge of the table, turning the fork through a right angle and inserting it into the open mouth. The fork has then to be withdrawn and lowered in the reverse way before being used to spear the next bit of food. For the British cadets these odd customs were irksome and galling and they were undoubtedly a contributory factor to the trouble that arose later in the camp when we were all put under close arrest.

Our main task at Lakeland was to learn to fly a United States Army Primary Training Aircraft, built by Stearman, and known to us as the PT 17. It was a biplane like the Tiger Moth, but chunkier, very sturdy and with a 220 hp radial engine. On 9 July I met my instructor for the first time. His name was E. A. Baker and at this first confrontation he assured me at once that he did not like 'the goddam British' and he was only going through the mortification of training me because his government had ordered him to do so. The acidulated voice from the front seat kept me on my toes, however, and I just longed for the day when I would be able to take this tough, well-powered aircraft up alone.

Like a homing pigeon I began to familiarize myself with the terrain over which I was learning to fly. There were lakes and orange groves, highways and rivers, the townships of Lakeland and Plant City and the Singing Tower at Lake Wales standing among moss-hung pines and flowering shrubs. One's second solo, even in a new type of aircraft, is not as traumatic an experience as the first. It took place on a glorious sub-tropical day. As I flew over the serried ranks of orange trees and banked above the silver lakes I had a marvellous sense of freedom. I sang 'The Battle Hymn of the Republic' out loud, something that I occasionally do even now when I am driving alone in the car.

There was little spare time at Lakeland but what there was was precious. A few miles to the east of Lakeland is the town of Bartow where I met Mary Sand and her husband. Families living in the district used to send invitations to the camp for cadets from the air school to join them for Sunday lunch. I was indeed fortunate to draw the name of Mary Sand. She introduced me not only to the real Florida and some of its finest wild places but also to the sensitive writing of Marjorie Kinnan Rawlings. Mary gave me a copy of *Cross Creek* which described the lives of five families living between Lochloosa and Orange Lake near Gainesville. The book provides a remarkable portrait of Florida more than thirty years ago. Marjorie Rawlings's home at Cross Creek is now a State museum. I have only to dip into her book to reawaken the bird voices, the strange summer fogs, the storms, the extreme humidity – which if you bent to tie up a shoelace was enough to bathe you at once in sweat, the doomlike atmosphere before the rains came and the freshness afterwards, the blossoms of golden allamanda, Florida flame vine, red wood lily and blazing hibiscus.

I never stopped marvelling at the variety of flowers and the wildlife. Around Lakeland the citrus groves used to echo with the sad notes of mourning doves saying 'Noah! Pay me! Pay me!' and with the gentle moaning of sparrow-sized ground doves. Tiny bobwhite quail used to call near Lake Parker and many pairs of noisy killdeer plover nested on the airfield. There were red-bellied woodpeckers, vireos, crested flycatchers and Carolina wrens in the trees and bushes, while ruby-throated hummingbirds swung on invisible wires to poise, motionless save for their vibrating wings, in front of the lovely hibiscus flowers. I sometimes saw red-tailed and duck hawks near the flying school while black and turkey vultures used to soar above the citrus groves. Several times turkey vultures actually joined me when I was flying at about 4000 feet. I used to cut the engine and glide silently downwards in formation with these much superior exponents of the art of flying. On my 21st birthday I was able to approach a magnificent bald eagle gliding and soaring near Plant City. Back on the ground I was very attracted by the prairie of Kissimmee which stretched south towards the Everglades. This was very much a land of palmetto, savannah and wide-open skies; here I saw the burrowing owl and the rare Florida crane whose trumpetings William Bartram in the 1770s called 'seraphic music in the ethereal skies'.

It was in April 1513 that Ponce de León came ashore and named this land Florida. The Sunshine State has many faces but it is famous for its springs of crystal water that bubble and gush upwards from subterranean limestone rivers. There is Silver Springs near Ocala with its alligators, Wakulla where I saw the rare limpkins, or rail-cranes, and Kissingen, which provided me with such life birds as the black-and-white wood ibis, the least bittern and the American egret. Today visitors gather in Cypress Gardens near Winterhaven for the aquashows and to watch long-limbed girls in bikinis. The tourists of today demand fast motor-boats but in 1942 this was a quiet chain of lagoons, disturbed only by the gentle hum of electric boats. Spreading live-oaks stood draped in their tresses of Spanish moss. Here in a steady fusion of water, undergrowth and hot sun, oily-green vines and ferns rampaged through a jungle of palms, exotic shrubs and cypress trees whose gnarled and grey-brown knees stood up stark above the pools. Tufted titmice called 'peter-peter' and mockingbirds declaimed their strident phrases. It was idyllic and the effect was heightened by huge swallow-tailed butterflies beating up and down in the sunlight. There was one secluded waterway which I explored many times. It was narrow, overhung and rank, but it formed a refuge for water turkeys, or anhingas, which used to swim with their serpent-like necks protruding from the water, and for purple gallinules, herons, egrets, shy wood duck and noisy boat-tailed grackles. Water moccasins, or cottonmouth snakes, with their deadly venom were quite common and I watched them swimming in streams close to the camp. There were also some small tree-dwelling lizards, called green anoles, which used to hop about the trunks and change colour rather like chameleons.

One of my favourite expeditions was to the Gulf Coast. In summer the Gulf of Mexico was too warm for daylight swimming. My great relaxation was to swim at night in the phosphorescent waters at Passagrille and then refresh myself with a Cuba Libre – a rum and coke in an iced glass. Not far away was Tarpon Springs and some interesting mudflats where in autumn I watched migrant waders such as dowitchers, stilts, least and semi-palmated sandpipers as well as laughing and Bonaparte's gulls and terns, including common, least, royal and Forster's. Brown pelicans were everywhere but the white pelican with a nine-foot wingspan was rather uncommon.

By now I had become fairly familiar with the PT 17. On the afternoon of 5 August I taxied out a strange machine which I had not flown before. I turned into wind on the airfield, opened the throttle and began to trundle across the grass. As I gathered speed, the tail plane came up, but I could not increase the speed. The ground was flashing past me but there was not enough lift to take off. Already I could see the perimeter fence beginning to move towards me. I pulled the control column back but the machine would not leave the ground. By now I was travelling too fast to brake and stop the aircraft before I reached the wire. I leaned back in my seat, trying to will the nose off the ground. As the fence rushed towards me like an express train I felt a slight stickiness in the controls.

The PT 17 lifted and cleared the wire by four feet. Slowly the aircraft staggered up to a height of about forty feet and I began a long, slow circle round into wind and landed back on the airfield.

Meanwhile the flying was becoming more testing and enjoyable with snap rolls, loops and free aerobatics. One day during a period of dual flying Baker suddenly cut the engine at 4000 feet without warning and laconically announced 'Engine failure! Forced landing!'

I looked ahead and over the side of the aircraft. A faint drift of smoke near Tampa gave me the wind direction, but there was nothing within reach of a gliding approach but woods, lakes and citrus groves. I had to make a decision. Below me the State Highway was running parallel to the direction of the wind and it was empty – Glory Be! I prepared my approach as I steadily lost height. After several wide gliding sweeps to lose the rest of the altitude, I made my downwind approach. I turned through ninety degrees to port, glided half a mile on the crosswind leg and banked the PT 17 through another right angle. I was now only a hundred feet up. The highway was still miraculously free of traffic and I began my final descent. With the machine floating only twenty feet above the roadway, Baker yelled, 'OK! Get this thing out of here!'

Florida often undergoes tremendous rains, storms and even tornadoes. The local people say that only fools and strangers ever try to forecast the weather. One afternoon not long after I had taken off for a solo flight, the empty cerulean sky started to fill, without warning and very quickly, with white cumulus clouds that boiled upwards like huge, menacing cauliflowers. I was flying at 2000 feet and at once decided to make for the airfield as quickly as possible. The next thing that I knew was that the PT 17 was being borne rapidly upwards as if in a lift. As soon as I realized that I had been caught in a great rising column of air, I opened the throttle and shoved the stick hard forwards. I should now have started a dramatic screaming dive towards the ground, but instead I was lifted up for almost another thousand feet. I had a feeling of total helplessness; then I finally broke away from the turbulent face and flew back to Lakeland. That day only half a dozen machines got back to the airfield; the rest came down in fields, groves and even on the State Highway! The dust storm was terrific and an old Florida character told me, 'Yep! It's a dust storm. There's only one sure way to tell it from a blow-up. You take a rabbit up to the first floor of the house and throw it out of the window. If it falls to the ground then it's only a blow-up. If it starts to burrow at once, it's a dust storm!'

We had strict orders not to fly near the Everglades, so I never saw them from the air, but I did venture out into *Pay-hay-okee* – the Seminole Indian name which meant 'grassy waters'. From the ground the view is one of waterways, islands, jungles, sawgrass prairies, hammocks, and in the evening quite superb sunsets, over the forests of mangrove. Here I saw garfish, alligators and turtles, night, Louisiana and little blue herons, roseate spoonbills, ibises, swallow-tailed kites and countless banded zebra butterflies. Today the water flow has been changed and disastrous droughts and ensuing fires have damaged one of North America's greatest natural assets. Carl W. Bucheister, President Emeritus of the Audubon Society in America, talked very pessimistically in 1971 in a World Service radio programme that I presented about the future of the 'Glades.

I remember my stay in Florida for many reasons. There was the flying, of course. The humidity and high temperature gave me prickly heat and a lasting memento of my visit. There was also the mystery of a military system devised as far as I could see to diminish the individual and even reduce him to stammering ineptitude. I can still hear the strident, arrogant shout of 'Well, mister?', directed by some Upperclassman at a junior cadet. I was assured by an American major travelling to Britain with me on the *Queen Elizabeth* in 1943 that such a system was designed to 'shape up' new American recruits who had had little or no discipline at home or school. Years later I retold the story on the air to Jack de Manio in his weekly programme.

But there were many compensating delights for which I shall always be grateful. Even in that great human playground of the American Continent there was a fascinating world of nature where, in my day, the earth, to quote Marjorie Rawlings, was 'borrowed but not bought'.

Aged three with my mother, Thomas *left*, Wilfrid and Margaret, 1924

With my mother, Thelma and father at Badby, 1950

The Cottage, Ladbroke Square, 1934

With three friends on top of the Empire State Building, New York, 1942

Wedding day, 23 December 1943. St Paul's, Oxgate

The crew of Q-Queenie 2, 626 Squadron, Wickenby, 1944. (*From left*: Paddy O'Meara, Bob Bond, Dick Tredwin, Johnny Neilson, ES, Bill Freeman, Pip Phillips)

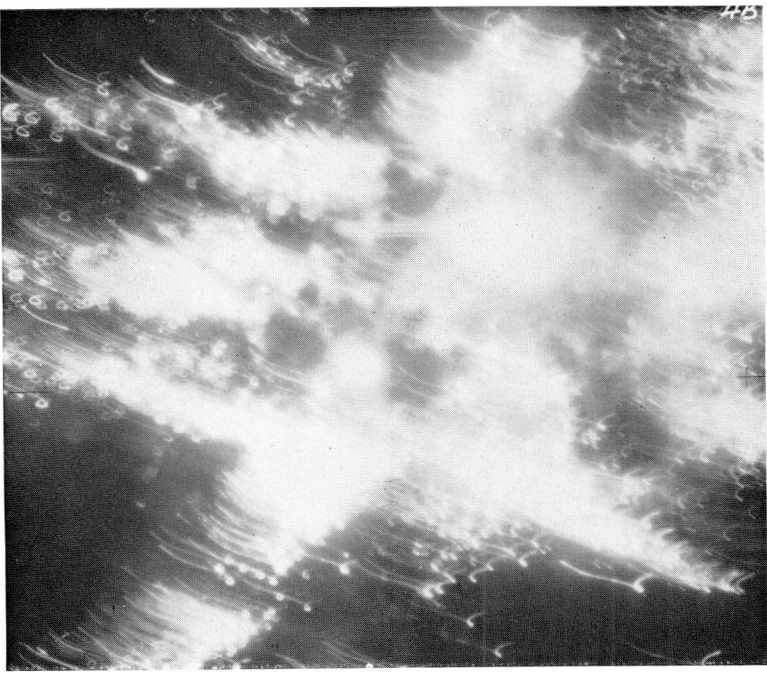

The photograph that I took of Essen just after we had been struck by six bombs, 26 April 1944

Left Setting up a three-foot diameter parabolic reflector to record birds. Buckinghamshire, 1957

Below Operating an 18-inch reflector with Bob Wade in our portable boat *Puffin*. Buckinghamshire, 1957

Right Stone curlew at nest

Below right Hen golden eagle feeding eaglet

Left Siamese kittens being recorded for a radio play for which I provided sound effects, 1954

Below Badgers feeding in front of parabolic microphone at night. Surrey, 1953

Right With Thelma, Joan and George Burton in the Prospect of Whitby, 1954

Below right The Hilbre Group, 1957. (*From left*: Ronnie Pryor, ES, Dr. Grant McAfee, Bill Wilson, Dorothy Hosking, Joe Wells, Lord Alanbrooke, Eric Hosking, John Parrinder)

Percy Thrower showing how to make a miniature garden in my *Collecting from Nature* television series, January 1961

With the late James Fisher in a television programme about birds, April 1958

6

From the Deep South to the Great Lakes

Just outside the city of Montgomery in Alabama lies the airbase of Gunter Field. In 1942 it was an American basic flying school and it was to this airfield that the graduates of Class 43A from Lakeland were posted early in September that year. Waiting for us were neat rows of squat, low-wing monoplanes, known as BT 13s, powered by 440 hp radials and with a top speed of about 156 mph. To me at least the aircraft seemed heavy and a bit underpowered.

The countryside over which I was now flying was very different from that of the citrus groves and silver lakes of Florida. From the air Montgomery spread smudgily across the brown and rather dirty Alabama river. There were harsh fields of sandy red earth, bordered by tiny hedges and sometimes by the brown-grey patches of woods showing up like a daub across an artist's oils. Close to the soil huddled the dust-grey hovels of the Negroes and the whole land from the air looked helpless and beaten. The streets of Montgomery – and Birmingham too – were shabby and neglected. Every bar and store, however tiny, was provided with two entrances, one marked 'White' and the other 'Black'. Montgomery was an army town and soldiers drifted disconsolately from bar to bar; it had little attraction for me. We did not fly every day, but the ground work was fairly demanding and we were given only ten hours of freedom at the weekend.

With a friend of mine, Mick Barron, and two American cadets we hired a Dodge to drive 180 miles to Atlanta – as far as Manchester is from London – and back in ten hours. Queues of people lined the long islands in the streets, waiting for buses, the women in striped and floral dresses just below the knee and the men in white caps or Panamas. *Holiday Inn* was showing at one cinema which also displayed the notice 'Enlist Today in Your Navy'. The voice of Dinah Shore floated out from the entrance of a crowded, smoky bar. After the Civil War Atlanta was rebuilt and in 1942 it was a relaxed city of white pre-skyscraper blocks and avenues surrounded by typical suburban houses and woods of pine. The aerial walkways, courtyards and plexiglas domes of Peachtree Street were yet to come.

Less than three weeks after I started flying at Gunter Field I woke up one morning with a severe ache in both my cheeks and also below my eyebrows. For the first and only time I reported sick in America. The verdict? – that I was suffering from sinusitis, and this condition was to plague me on and off for many years to come. I was grounded from flying for a week. After a flight with an American captain I was told that it would not be possible for me to catch up the time lost and so I was being taken off the course. This was a shattering blow.

For five weeks at Gunter I had been sharing a barrack room with Alan Skempton, whom I had first met at the start of the pilot's course. I was to meet and know him again when he was a much respected BBC news reader and announcer. Alan was a quiet, cultured man, rather shy by nature, cherishing a few close friends and not over-enamoured of the noisy, extrovert way of life in the service. I liked him very much and was saddened by his early death in 1969. When he heard of my elimination from the course he said quietly and with understanding in his voice, 'These things often work out for the best!' and with the gift of hindsight I am sure that he was right.

Now my service career was to change course. I was posted to Trenton in Ontario where I would be able to opt for another aircrew category. The journey north was a long one. The temperature dropped from the eighties in Alabama to below freezing in Canada, which was ablaze with the scarlet and gold of dying maple leaves. I decided to become an air bomber and for this I needed another five months of bombing, gunnery and navigation training in Canada with some opportunities for actually flying aircraft at a later stage.

But first I was granted leave. My pay at this time as an LAC in the RAF was not very high, unlike the American cadets who

From the Deep South to the Great Lakes

had been paid small fortunes. I wanted to see New York, so I decided that there was only one way to do it – by hitch-hiking! I managed to reach Toronto and there I flagged down an enormous aluminium-coloured lorry belonging to the Consolidated Truck Company. The cabin of this giant truck was fitted out with a rest-bed, coffee machine and radio and I could see that I was going to have a very comfortable ride. The truck-driver – 'Call me Hank!' – was a quiet introspective man on his way to Albany. He was a most sympathetic and informative guide to southern Canada and the north-eastern United States.

Our route took us across the Lakes Peninsula to Hamilton, east to Buffalo with its port and shipyards, and across the States to the car city of Syracuse, Utica, Schenectady and finally into Albany, the capital of New York State, which lay ten miles below the confluence of the Hudson and Mohawk Rivers. I had travelled 450 miles in comfort – a very good first hop. My place high up in the cabin of the truck had given me a fine view of the passing scene and with stops in cafés I had been granted a rewarding transect of American life. We arrived in the truck depot at half past two in the morning. The manager insisted that as an Allied serviceman I should be given a free supper and the T-bone steak, apple pie and ice-cream were very welcome. Hank took me across to another table in the canteen and introduced me to Joe, another driver, who was going to make the run for New York in half an hour's time.

My new companion was an easy-going New Yorker who was quite pleased to have someone with him on his drive down the Hudson River. Dawn cast a long low gleam from the east across the Catskill Mountains and a Cooper's hawk crossed the road in a powerful glide. I saw the name Hyde Park on the map and leaned forward in the cab in the hope of getting a view towards the Hudson of President Roosevelt's home. The road was now becoming increasingly bordered by strips of bungalows, shacks, sheds and billboards. Joe said, 'This is the beginning of New York,' and I naively answered, 'But I don't see any skyscrapers!'

I was told that we were still fifteen miles from Manhattan and the traditional New York skyline. The dingy and depressing suburb through which we were passing was called Yonkers. I had not yet discovered that the finest view of the skyscrapers is from New York Bay.

At the junction of 42nd Street and Fifth Avenue the truck pulled up.

'This OK?' demanded Joe. And then, 'When are you coming back?'

'In six days' time,' I replied.

'Be here at the junction of Fifth and 42nd at 2.30 on Thursday afternoon and I'll pick you up. Don't be late!'

I said goodbye to Joe and, like a turnstone at the foot of Conachair's massive sea-precipice on St Kilda, I set out to get my bearings, among the man-made cliffs. Grand Central Terminal was only two blocks away and Times Square and theatreland lay just to the west. I booked in at the YMCA where for only about 1s 6d a night I was provided with my own clean, well-furnished room and breakfast. After visiting the USO – the American Services Organizations – I was issued with enough dinner and theatre tickets, free of charge, to last the whole of my stay.

I explored New York both on foot and by the Metro, which I thought was behind the London Tubes in comfort and modernity. It is strange to recall now that the most nostalgic sound in America for us was that of another cadet shouting 'Mind the doors!' I walked up Broadway to see Times Square and to collect a periodic free glass of Pepsi-cola from their advertising bar.

With my USO meal tickets I dined out at very good restaurants in the evenings. One night, before going on to a show, I went into a bar near Eighth Avenue and ordered a whisky sour. A few paces away sitting alone on a stool was a blonde girl whose face was familiar. Suddenly it dawned on me – I had last seen that face together with those of Judy Garland and Mickey Rooney on a cinema screen in Harrow.

'Excuse me! Are you not June Preisser?'

Yes, it was the lively and acrobatic girl who had starred in the 1939 MGM musical *Babes in Arms*, directed by the 'geometric choreographer' Busby Berkeley. She was most interested to know what was happening in Europe and felt that Americans could have little idea as they were so far from the battle.

It was the concentrated and synthetic heart of Manhattan – the traditional area of towers and skyscrapers – that commanded one's attention. It was here that Le Corbusier had exclaimed, 'Good God! What disorder, what impetuosity!' A silent lift carried three cadets and myself to the top of the Empire State Building. From our sunny eyrie more than a thousand feet above the dark chasms of Manhattan, where light rarely penetrated, we looked down on the other skyscrapers – the stark white Rockefeller Center and the metallic spire of the Chrysler Building. Far below, the ribbon of Fifth Avenue ran north and straight as a die to Central Park.

Back at street level once more, I walked along Fifth Avenue to the Rockefeller Center – a great commercial adventure of the inter-war period. I visited Radio City with its famous music hall where I saw the Rockettes in action – that fabulous troupe of dancers whose precision and timing were a delight to watch. Times Square at night was aglow with neon lights, displays, huge billboards and the moving band of light that flashed up the latest news bulletins. New York was also alive in 1942 with all-night movies and strip clubs, called burlesque shows, which ran continuous performances of arid and tasteless entertainment – a foretaste of what the future was to bring many years later to Soho. But there was the Hayden Planetarium and that Aladdin's cave of wonders – the American Museum of Natural History – with its 800 000 birds, including those wren-like birds – *Traversia lyalli* – discovered on Stephen Island in Cook Strait, New Zealand, by the lighthouse keeper's cat, which carried home nearly a dozen examples before the supply dried up for ever.

No. 31 Bombing and Gunnery School, Picton, where I started my course, lay on a peninsula jutting out into Lake Ontario. Our gunnery exercises were carried out in Fairchild-built Blenheims, called Bolingbrokes, from whose hydraulic turrets we fired Vickers gas-operated guns. For the wind-finding and bombing exercises we flew in Ansons, designed to carry a crew of three. In some of them the undercarriage had to be wound up by hand after take-off and I remember clearly how tedious this used to be with something like 126 turns before the wheels locked in the up position. For bombing we used a hand-held bombsight for low-level attacks and a Mk IX course-setting bombsight for high level. The pilot flew the Anson and altered his course on instructions from the air bomber so that the aircraft tracked correctly over the target. It was very much a team operation.

As the autumn at Picton moved into winter the snows came and the weather became very cold. Huge machines were employed to blow the snow off the field so that we could fly; this was specialized equipment that I had not seen in England. Deep snow covered the countryside and twenty-foot-long icicles hung down along the roads. We lived in wooden huts, faced with shingles, and these were quite incredibly well heated by furnaces fed on air-blown coal dust. The area was quite devoid of birds.

In February 1943 I moved to No. 31 Air Navigation School at Port Albert, near Goderich, on Lake Huron. Our flying exercises in Ansons were concentrated now on map reading, reconnaissance, simulated bombings on infra-red targets that left traces on sensitive plates and photography, while the ground work was devoted to navigation exercises, aircraft recognition – bird-watching helped me here! – and practical signals. It was clear that this course was preparing us for many tasks and situations. We also learned to operate the F 24 camera, taking vertical pinpoint photographs of selected targets or leaning out of Ansons to take oblique shots of the snow-bound Ontario landscape. As the final examination approached, I retreated to the chapel where I could study in peace. I passed and was offered a commission and the dubious honour of escorting a number of new sergeant bomb aimers across Canada.

On 2 April we left Moncton by rail for Halifax and once again I heard that sad tremulous sound of a train whistle on the North American continent – a sound that I had listened to on many nights as it drifted across the lowland plains from the Deep South to Novia Scotia. Awaiting us in Halifax was no cross-channel boat like the *Banfora*, but instead the *Queen Elizabeth* in grey wartime paint. The *Queen* made good speed across the Atlantic, without escort, and each mile of water covered brought us nearer to the war in Europe.

From the Deep South to the Great Lakes

We steamed slowly up the Firth of Clyde. On the port side lay green hills and fields from Toward Point to Loch Long. It was an ethereal green – that of spring in Britain – a green that I had not seen since May 1942. Nowhere in Canada or the United States did the landscape bear this fresh colour among its browns, golds, bronzes and dark greens. This was the colour of home. After being kitted up at Harrogate with my officer's uniform, tin hat and respirator, I went home to Appleby to spend three weeks with my mother and father among the fresh morning air of the fells. I was home and for a while it was good to be alive.

7

The War Comes Closer

By a curious stroke of good fortune I was posted, actually on the day after 617 Squadron's famous raid on the Dams, to do my advanced training at No. 2 (O) AFU at Millom in Cumberland. As the crow flies this was about forty miles from Appleby and so I would be able to visit my parents at Castle Bank on forty-eight-hour passes and at weekends. The airfield at Millom lay on the southern tip of a broad triangular peninsula. Although the skyline with the rocky mass of Black Combe to the north, high fells to the north-east and water on two sides was attractive enough, Millom was a characterless industrial town.

At Millom I flew with different staff pilots on more advanced gunnery, bombing and navigation exercises. Once I flew over Appleby and had a perfect view of Castle Bank and my mother in the garden. About three weeks after I had arrived at Millom I was posted without warning to No. 1 Air Armament School at Manby in Lincolnshire. Here I found myself on a three weeks' course with five other officers on the new Mark XIV bombsight with which Bomber Command was largely to be equipped. It was the first 'tactically free' sight and was fitted to Blenheim IVs from which we dropped our eight-and-a-half pound practice bombs on ranges off the Lincolnshire coast where clouds of gulls and waders used to get up on our approach. The engines fitted to the Blenheims were Bristol Mercury radials that had a tendency to overheat before take off. I had one hair-raising flight when an engine cut on take off and the second began to misfire so that we found ourselves switchbacking over the Lincolnshire countryside at only 150 feet while we swept round in a flat curve to make a landing back at Manby. Another Blenheim lost power on take-off in the same way and plunged into a petrol bowser and tea van, killing four people.

On 13 July 1943 I packed my kitbags and made the journey south to Oxfordshire. A service truck collected me at Upper Heyford station and bore me off to No. 16 Operational Training Unit (OTU) where I was to meet the other aircrew categories that would form my crew. It was a warm and sunny day; the elms were dark and oily green in their summer livery and the roadsides were drifts of white hogweed, purple vetch and golden lady's bedstraw. As the truck climbed up the dusty, aromatic road to a flat plateau of land, a dark cigar-shaped aircraft with two radial engines passed low overhead on its noisy approach to the airfield. This was a Vickers Wellington bomber, or 'Wimpy' as it was affectionately known after Popeye's cartoon friend, T. Wellington Wimpy. It was one of the greatest and most successful warplanes of the Second World War. It was built from an immensely strong criss-cross design of metal ribs, known as geodetic construction and devised by Barnes Wallis of the R.100 airship and the dambusting bomb.

The first part of the course consisted of ground training and I was then despatched to Barford St John, but this time as a member of a crew. One day all the aircrew were assembled to form their crews. Navigators, bomb aimers, gunners and wireless operators wandered round, slightly embarrassed in some cases, catching the eye of a pilot or some other member of aircrew and offering to join up. In some instances old friends had been rediscovered and many aircrew had already formed an idea of the pilots with whom they wished to fly. At this stage I had provisionally arranged to join a Chilean pilot, Tom Wheat, as his bomb aimer. However, Wing Commander G. Lowe, the Officer Commanding the Training Wing, intervened to introduce to me another wing commander, Philip Haynes, who had just come from the post of T. 1 Armament at Bomber Command to fly on operations. The newcomer was a regular officer with past service on the North-West Frontier and in other parts of the world. He was a suave, shrewd and courteous man, who, after the introductions were over, quietly said, 'I would be very pleased if you would be willing to fly with me.

I know that you have chosen to fly with someone else but I am forming a crew and I would like you to be a member of it.'

I began by saying that I would have to ask Tom Wheat to release me, as a matter of courtesy, and this Tom was willing to do. I liked the forthrightness of Philip Haynes's approach and after I had finally made up my mind to join him I never once regretted it. Later that year he was to establish the new 626 Squadron at Wickenby as its first Commanding Officer.

Also at Philip's invitation to join our crew came Sergeant W. (Bill) Freeman as navigator, Sergeant R. (Bob) Bond as wireless operator, Sergeant Kevin (Paddy) O'Meara from Eire as rear gunner and Flying Officer R. H. T. (Dick) Tredwin as mid-upper gunner. Dick Tredwin, who was staff instructor at Upper Heyford, had already completed a first tour of thirty operations on Short Stirlings – 'Queens of the Sky', he used to call them. But he was anxious to do a second tour of twenty operations as soon as possible. Philip had picked his crew with care, searching for aspects of character that appealed to him as well as consulting proficiency assessments. The experience of living and flying with these outstanding companions was different in kind from any other associations that I formed later in life.

Shortly after my arrival at Barford St John I became aware of a dark hangar on the far side of the airfield. I also discovered that it was regarded as our bounden duty, on seeing a strange aircraft, to stand with our back to it until it had passed. One day I was cycling along the perimeter track where it curved round the edge of a small wood and, as I rounded the corner, there right in front of me was the strangest-looking aircraft that I had ever seen. It was streamlined and its wheels were almost hidden in two 'propellerless' engine nacelles so that it sat very close to the ground. Its tail plane was rooted in a pod halfway up the fin and rudder. I was looking at one of the prototype F 9/40s – the famous Gloster Meteors. Its chief test pilot at Barford St John was Michael Daunt, who had also flown the first jet aircraft – the E 28/39 Pioneer, made possible by the research into jet propulsion by Air Commodore Sir Frank Whittle.

The War Comes Closer

One day, after flying was over, I was having a drink with Michael in the mess at Barford and he enquired, 'Have you been up today?'

'Yes,' I replied, 'it was very clear too. Visibility wasn't bad from 4000 feet.'

In quiet tones he added, 'It wasn't bad from 42 000!'

The countryside around Barford St John was a very English one, with brown stone villages, quiet inns, rolling cornfields and copses rich in yellowhammer songs. Adderbury, with its gracious Georgian houses, handsome church and greens, was within easy reach even by service bicycle, and there was always the Black Boy at Milton for refreshment on the way. There was an aroma of high summer along the fields and roads, in pleasant contrast to the smell of metal, hot oil and aviation fuel.

An event occurred at Adderbury which was to shape the rest of my life. On the evening of 10 August a staff friend of mine at Barford, Flying Officer Jack Buchanan, and I decided to cycle over to that village for a drink in the Red Lion. As we walked in, we could see Philip Haynes was sitting having a drink with a vivacious WAAF officer whom I had not seen before. 'Ah, Eric!' exclaimed the Wing Commander, beckoning me over. 'Allow me to introduce you to Section Officer Thelma Jackson – the Queen Bee at Barford. What'll you have – a pint, I suppose?' We had a most entertaining evening and I was aware that something out of the ordinary had happened. Thelma, who was the WAAF Commanding Officer at Barford St John, had only just returned from leave, which was why I had not seen her before. What had happened was so special that we have celebrated that first evening on which we met on every succeeding 10 August.

I proposed in the garden of the WAAF Officers' Mess at Heyford and on my birthday on 24 August we became engaged. Section Officer Kay Roberts, the Code and Cypher officer, gave a birthday party in the mess and announced our news. Thelma's sister, Jeanne, who was a corporal in the motor transport section at RAF Longside, near Peterhead in Aberdeenshire, came on leave and stayed in Bloxham. On 3 September the three of us and Jack Buchanan went into Oxford for a meal. To our great astonishment and delight the church bells began to ring to celebrate the armistice signed between Italy and the Allies. That same day the British landed at Reggio in Calabria and the news was deceptively reassuring.

The climax of our operational training came on 15 September when Philip Haynes took us in Wellington III 612 'D-DOG' on a leaflet raid to France. This operation was known by the code name of 'Nickel'. The aiming point was the village of La Flèche on the Loir and some twenty-five miles southwest of Le Mans. The leaflets carried the legend *Recommandations importantes aux sans-filistes français* and gave advice on how to receive BBC broadcasts and what precautions to take. As we crossed the French coast we could see searchlights probing the sky over Le Havre and spasmodic flashes from the flak batteries in the harbour. The photograph that I took with the aid of a photoflash showed I had dropped the leaflets on target. On the way back the skipper reported a loss of oil pressure on the port engine and I went back to work the Zwicky pump handle, but it was difficult for Philip to maintain height. As we descended on our effective engine, it was clear that we would have to try to land at the first airfield in England. Philip called up Tangmere to get clearance for an emergency landing and here we came down safely just before midnight. Thelma had gone to the Heyford flying control tower to welcome us back, but it was not possible for us to make contact with Heyford for several hours. We thus became overdue and missing at base. It was, I am glad to say, the first and only time!

In October Philip Haynes and his crew were posted to No. 1656 Conversion Unit at Lindholme and here we were joined by the last member of our crew, a very experienced flight engineer, Flight Lieutenant H. B. (Pip) Phillips. He was to play a vital role in the four-engined aircraft we were about to fly. Here at Lindholme we were introduced to the Avro Lancaster, that remarkable flying machine which Marshal of the RAF Sir Arthur Harris called 'the greatest single factor in winning the war'.

The bomb aimer had quite an adventurous journey from the entrance hatch near the tail to the nose. I had to negotiate the step up on to the flight deck, clamber over two main spars. In the summer in full flying kit and Mae West and weighed down with guns and other impedimenta I used to arrive sweating and then, after take off, get progressively colder as we gained height. To enter the nose compartment I climbed through a low square hole and over and down a step. Above and behind me were the pilot's and flight engineer's positions. In front of me was the Lancaster's nose – a great perspex bubble fitted with an angled flat glass panel that prevented distortion of ground details; this helped with map-reading and the sighting of the bombsight on the run-up to a target. My normal position was prone on a large green cushion placed over the forward escape hatch in the floor of the Lanc. Above me was the front turret into which I could climb and which held two .303 Browning machine-guns. Between me and the perspex bubble was a small backward-facing chute for dropping bundles of 'Window' – the code name for strips of metallized paper dropped to confuse the enemy's radar defences. It was of special interest to me that one of the original inventors of 'Window' was H. W. B. Gill, Emeritus Fellow, and, during my stay at Merton, the domestic bursar there.

Having settled myself in the nose, I was free to look around. On my right was the bomb aimer's panel. At the top was a switch for the 4000-pound-bomb slip heater which was there to prevent the bomb, known as a 'cookie', from hanging up through icing. In practice, Bob Bond used to report that the big bomb had gone as the slip cover was near his position where he sat among his transmitters, receivers, amplifiers and monitors. There was a dim lamp, controlled by a rheostat, to illuminate the panel. Under the lamp was a master switch and individual switches for fusing the bombs live. There were controls for the F 24 camera and the photoflash. At the extreme left-hand side was a double row of eight bomb-selector switches and a panel to regulate the dropping of bombs in sticks and the time intervals between them. A long selector box was also provided for establishing the order in which the bombs fell away from the Lancaster's thirty-three-foot-long bomb bay so that the aircraft remained balanced in flight. The actual bomb-release button was kept in a special stowage position with a guard above it to prevent pressing the tit at the wrong time. There was also a mounting for the Mk XIV bombsight computer box, while the sighting head, marked 'Handle Like Eggs!' was fitted above the clear glass panel.

We were now a highly trained and very fit crew. The cost of training each member was of the order of £10 000, enough to send ten men to Oxford or Cambridge for three years. I spent many hours playing squash with Philip and managed to run a few competition half-miles. We were all keyed up for the testing time ahead. For two whole years I had been training for this moment. But what were the real implications? It was clear what the role of Bomber Command was – to bomb! I was quite well aware of the expected role of this great bomber fleet, created by the War Cabinet and the Chiefs of Staff, who themselves knew perfectly well that women and children would die whenever it went into action. But in 1943 how were we placed in Britain? There was no immediate prospect of a Second Front and there were few ways open to us to try to limit Germany's strength in armaments and economic growth. It was the Casablanca Conference which had laid down in January 1943 the basic strategy for the bomber offensive – 'the progressive destruction and dislocation of the German military, industrial and economic system, and the undermining of the morale of the German people to a point where their capacity for armed resistance is fatally weakened'. These were ambitious words and if it were capable of being achieved then there was an argument in its favour; in the autumn of 1943 no one could say that it would fail. I was brought up to believe that killing and war were abhorrent and this is still my belief, but I also hated Nazism and its special tyranny.

Area bombing was not discussed in our early training and we had understood that it would be our task to reach defined targets and hit them as accurately as we could. Only on 'ops' did we discover the true limitations of the offensive. One could only make a judgement in 1943 on what it was reasonable to believe at the time and not on hindsight and the verdict of history. In Britain there was, as I recall, a popular welcome – even demand – for the growing bomber offensive which was the only way in which we could put pressure on our enemy. We in Bomber Command would have much preferred to live and enjoy our youth, but we held that Nazism must not be allowed to triumph, especially as we had lost our chance to contain it in the 1930s. This was one of the reasons why German civilians died in the war. I know at least that the destruction of life and property in the Third Reich for which I was directly responsible was in the cause of victory and not for the sake of destruction alone. I am quite clear that given the same circumstances and knowledge as existed in 1943 I would not have acted differently.

8

The Air Assault on Europe

On 3 November 1943 the Air Officer Commanding-in-Chief, Bomber Command, Sir Arthur Harris told the Prime Minister, Winston Churchill, that 'we can wreck Berlin from end to end if the USAAF will come in on it. It will cost between 400 – 500 aircraft. It will cost Germany the war.' He sincerely believed that this could be achieved with just the Lancaster bombers at his disposal, although the Deputy Chief of the Air Staff, Air Marshal Sir Norman Bottomley, favoured a more selective role for these aircraft; he thought that the precision bombing of vital centres of production would be more effective than area attacks. Be that as it may, it was with the C-in-C's minute hanging over our heads that we arrived in November at the No. 1 Group wartime station at Wickenby on the Lincolnshire Plain to begin our contribution to the air assault on Europe, and particularly Germany. Philip Haynes commanded the new 626 Squadron, which was formed by taking 'C' Flight from No. 12 Squadron, which was already based at Wickenby, and making it the new 'A' Flight of 626. 'B' Flight was to be commanded by a delightful New Zealand pilot, Squadron Leader J. D. (Johnny) Neilson, who was also to be our first pilot, as Philip would have many administrative duties although he intended to fly on operations whenever he could.

Aircraft of our new 626 Squadron bore the code letters UM. The Squadron motto 'To Strive and Not to Yield' was taken from Tennyson's line 'To Strive, To Seek, To Find and Not to Yield', which was also the epitaph of my boyhood heroes, Captain Scott, Dr Wilson and 'Birdie' Bowers lying in the desolation of the Antarctic. It was almost inevitable that the perfection of that line would be corrupted to 'To Press On

Regardless'. The crest bore a galley with seven oars to denote the seven members of aircrew.

I opened my tour of 'ops' with three raids on Berlin in five nights involving some twenty-four hours' flying, most of it over enemy territory. The organization of these raids was a very complex affair. At the highest level the War Cabinet instructed the Air Staff on matters of policy, while the day-to-day choice of targets and the planning of the operations were made at Bomber Command Headquarters at High Wycombe. Then the Command Operational Order was sent down to each Group Commander. The Air Officer Commanding No. 1 Group was Air Vice-Marshal E. A. B. Rice. He was a tolerant and likable South African, and a great supporter of 'Butch' Harris. His Group Headquarters were at Bawtry Hall where Thelma was later to be posted. The AOC then briefed the commanders at Base and the orders were passed on to Station and Squadron. Our base station was Ludford Magna and its commander Air Commodore R. S. Blucke, became the AOC of 1 Group in 1945. As the squadrons on the airfields learned that they would be operating that night, a kind of tremor used to move through the stations. Few knew the actual target. It was sufficient to have been told at this stage the number of aircraft required, the length of the flight and the type of bomb load needed.

Several hours before take-off we would go out to our aircraft, checking, examining and perhaps air-testing it. Then some of the airmen assembled for a pre-briefing to prepare flight plans and navigational charts. All of us gathered then in the briefing room. On my first operation I walked in, glanced up at the great wall map of Europe and followed the line of red ribbon that stretched in a series of straight legs to the target. Berlin! – the Big City – what a target to start on! Philip Haynes opens the proceedings with remarks about the target and any spoof raids or diversions that are also planned for the night. The intelligence officer reports on the factories and installations in the target area and on any decoys in the region. Then follow the specialist officers – navigation, bombing, signals, gunnery and engineering. The meterological officer hazards a forecast for the route and the target, with very little to go on, and is often greeted with a chorus of groans or cries of derision. If he is wildly out, he may well be rolled up in the mess carpet on our return! The Wing Commander sums up and the Station Commander wishes us luck.

Meanwhile from early in the morning the armourers have been taking out hundreds of four-pound incendiary bombs and high-explosive missiles from the bomb dump near Grange Farm. The small fire bombs have to be loaded into containers known as SBCs. Other men are wheeling out trolleys bearing 4000-pound cookies. Occasionally, when the weather changes over Europe and the target has to be altered, the Lancs have to be unloaded and a new set of bombs put on, sometimes in freezing weather and often in high wind and rain. One keen but over-anxious air bomber, who wanted to show the wireless operator in his crew how to release a 'cookie', if it was hung up over the target, took him into a bombed-up Lancaster which was standing in a dispersal with its bomb doors open. 'This is what you do!' he said. 'You push this lever forward and away it goes!' Unaware that the aircraft was bombed up, he pushed the lever forward. A second or so later a sickening thud below them announced that a 4000-pound bomb had just fallen on to the tarmac – without going off!

Giant petrol bowsers, each carrying 2500 gallons of aviation spirit, just 300 gallons more than each Lanc. can hold, have been running out to the parked bombers. Electricians check fuses, warning lights, equipment and deal with negative earths. The ground staff are older than the aircrews but as Stan Wells, who served at Wickenby recalls, their own allotted Lancaster 'was as much ours, of course, as the aircrew to whom she was assigned'.

For us in the aircrews, after our meal of bacon, eggs and very sugary tea, come some of the worst moments. We are about to leave the peaceful Lincolnshire countryside for some unknown future over Germany. In the long Nissen hut of the locker room I begin to dress, pulling over my battledress an inner flying suit full of kapok and then an outer suit. I put on socks, then electrically heated socks, and more socks and then I have to squeeze my feet into fleece-lined suède flying boots. I check that I have my silk and woollen gloves and my leather gauntlets. I put on my parachute harness and collect a parachute pack from a smart and cheerful WAAF. On top of the harness goes my yellow Mae West. I start to sweat and beads of perpiration run down my back. I pick up my helmet and oxygen mask, goggles, escape kit, thermos flask, orange juice in tins, chocolate, Horlicks tablets and my flimsy case. I console myself with a thought: 'Thank heavens I put the guns in the front turret this afternoon!' I roll out of the hut and into Johnny Neilson's little Standard truck. We drive halfway round the airfield to a brand-new Lancaster B III, parked on a small circle of concrete. Her name is 'Q-Queenie 2'.

It is just after half past three on a cool grey afternoon. There is time for a quick cigarette and a last relieving of nature before we clamber into the aircraft. I survive the journey forward cushioned by my flying suits against the knocks and bangs from the spars and metal corners. For take-off I stay out of my compartment. The starboard inner and then the rest of the Merlin engines turn, cough and fire. Pip goes through a cockpit check with Johnny and we roll forward in the half-light to join the queue of other Lancs on the perimeter track waiting for take-off. All the time we are keeping an eye on the deadline for take-off after which we must 'abort' if we are not airborne. Once a maximum effort was ruined when a flock of American Dakotas towing gliders flew low over the runway right in the middle of our take-off period.

At last our time comes and the great machine swings on to the runway. We have green light clearance for take-off and the four Merlins on full boost roar into life. The brakes are released and we lurch forward and begin to thunder down the concrete-and-asphalt strip. With a full bomb load – and Lancs in 1 Group were famous for the size of their loads – and maximum fuel the Lancaster is now very vulnerable and struggles to lift itself off from the ground – and there is very little margin for safety. At last she is up and I glimpse some tiny figures by the runway waving us farewell. Ahead I can see in the growing dusk the towers of Lincoln Cathedral which were many times to give us welcome and reassurance on our return from Europe. For a moment I pray, falling back on Sir Jacob Astley's prayer before the Battle of Edgehill. Now we begin to climb up towards other bombers assembling above the flat grey fields. I ease my way down into the nose compartment where I shall spend the next seven hours.

In the last of the upper daylight the sky seems to be filling with dark shapes struggling to reach their altitude before setting off eastwards to a rendezvous point out over the North Sea. We pass up through cloud and I can report nothing on the ground. Soon it is too dark to see the rest of the force as we reach the rendezvous point and set course for Hitler's Europe. 'Keep your eyes skinned, chaps!' comes the skipper's instruction. Paddy, Dick and I test our guns over the sea, but ammo is precious. Pip monitors the engine instruments and keeps an additional look-out. Over 10 000 feet we all go on to oxygen and then we settle at 23 000 for the trip ahead. What will it bring?

Bill Freeman is busily working away behind his curtains with his Gee set and his dead reckoning, alert for jamming by the Germans of his equipment; he gives quiet warnings and instructions to the skipper, for we only spoke in our crew when there was something to communicate – 'Keep on this course for another six minutes, skipper!', 'Turn on to 064 degrees magnetic!', 'ETA at target is . . .' and so on. Bob Bond, the wireless operator, works closely with Bill getting bearings, broadcast winds and time checks. 'Six minutes to the enemy coast!' comes the report from Bill. Now the adrenalin begins to flow more strongly, my muscles go taut and I have a slight pain in the lower abdomen. 'Enemy coast ahead!'–it is a phrase pregnant with meaning.

Suddenly, right in front of us, a pair of brilliant yellow target indicators dropped by the Pathfinders bursts and falls, illuminating the cloud below. Here is the crossing point and Bill has navigated us right on track as we fly between the glowing markers. Over on the port side orange bursts show up a defended area as the heavy flak guns begin to open up. There is everything to be said for a first-class navigator! We turn again. 'Eyes open for fighters!' comes the call from the skipper. I begin to push a packet of 'Window' out of the little chute every two minutes, a rate that will increase as we fly closer to the target. On our port side a flak burst glows in the dark, followed by another a little lower, and then the sky erupts into light as a bomber receives a direct hit and explodes in mid-air, fragments falling in a cascade of fire towards the ground. Off track he has received no benefit from the 'Window' cover and a radar-controlled battery easily gets his range. There can be no survivors.

Johnny flies the aircraft in a long series of turns, climbs and descents – manoeuvres known as 'corkscrewing' – a device to throw off pursuing fighters. We are now getting closer to Berlin. Paddy, having a cold, rough ride in the rear turret, reports on the flak behind and Dick keeps a visual sweep going above the aircraft while I peer back and down from time to time in the nose; there might be a fighter directly under us. At this time the Germans were using fighters to fly right under a bomber where, unobserved, they could fire vertically up with cannons at the engines and petrol tanks with devastating effect. 'Q-Queenie 2' with her great load of bombs and petrol, rides slowly through the night sky compared with the German night fighters. With our .303 Browning machine guns we are outranged and outgunned by our adversaries.

Now the flak is becoming intense and in my plastic dome I find myself being pushed through black clouds of smoke left by the fierce orange shell bursts. Sometimes I hear a dull thud as a round explodes rather too close. We move through a fantastic curtain of flame and smoke. I switch on the computer and the gyro in the bombsight. Zero hour is approaching and we are on the final leg into the target. I make a last check on all my switches and set the latest information from Bill on the bombsight computer. The thin air is turbulent with exploding shells and bombers' slipstreams. From out of the darkness a searing red cascade of fireworks – the first markers – begins to burn ahead of us, followed by another. Zero – minus five! The aircraft suddenly rocks as we catch the slipstream of a bomber in front.

I take command of the Lancaster as we run steadily into the target. 'Bomb doors open!' I call to the skipper. The flak is now savage as Berlin knows it will be the target for tonight. German fighters begin to drop brilliant flares along the bomber track and on both sides. A great bright flyway is laid out towards Germany's capital.

I take the bomb release switch out of its stowage and hold it in my right hand. Green target indicators go down and the aiming point is being marked. I peer through the glass of the Mk XIV bombsight head with its illuminated sword-shaped graticule and begin to instruct Johnny to fly to the aiming point – 'Left, left, steady . . . left a bit more . . . steady . . . steady . . . right a little . . . steady' and the bright green markers of the aiming point begin to slide smoothly down the long line of the graticule. 'Right a fraction . . . steady . . . steady!' There is a sudden bang and 'Q-Queenie 2' rocks violently as a shell bursts under the starboard wing. 'Right . . . right . . . steady now . . . steady!' The rest of the crew go through agonies of suspense as I grit my teeth for the final run-up. 'Steady . . . steady!' The intersecting lines of the graticule overlay the aiming point. I press the button. 'Bombs gone!' I shout, as the Lancaster, losing its load of bombs, surges upwards. 'Cookie gone!' reports Bob from the release slip. I check that there are no hang-ups in the bomb bay; this is especially important if any of the bombs are fitted with delayed-action fuses. 'Bomb doors closed!' I call, and Johnny takes back the Lancaster.

We run on over Berlin. It is a fantastic – an Homeric – sight! The air is a chaotic but beautiful mass of green and dying red markers, livid flak bursts, brilliant flares and long glowing streaks from lines of tracer bullets tearing towards their targets. A bomber explodes and flaming bits of debris drip slowly earthwards while another with blazing petrol tanks glides down to destruction like a giant meteor. Beneath the lurid show of pyrotechnics the cloud heaves with light as high-explosive bombs burst underneath, searchlights are switched on, the anti-aircraft batteries open fire and long rows of incendiaries begin to glow and catch. Bill emerges from behind his curtains, mutters an imprecation of disbelief and horror at what he sees and never again looks out at a target. Johnny goes on corkscrewing, for the bright clouds below will help the fighters to spot the bombers silhouetted against the brightness – the *Wilde Sau* system, as it was called. Another bomber appears as a long dying tongue of flame and Dick reports a fighter flashing past his turret.

In front of us is a long drag back across Fortress Europe,

carried out with an inevitable sense of anticlimax. We suffer from some reaction, but we cannot relax. Hot coffee, Horlicks tablets and chocolate begin to put new life into us. But my eyes are tired, my feet suddenly feel cold and the oxygen mask begins to smell strange. I go on peering into the darkness as I have done for the past three and a half hours. Thelma thought that we in Bomber Command always looked 'old about the eyes'. I go on peering, always peering. Fatigue affects us all but we sharpen our senses, change our positions. The long leg back could be more dangerous than the target itself.

At last the coast of Lincolnshire welcomes us as we come through the cloud once more. Johnny calls up flying control at Wickenby. 'Hullo, Grateful! This is Q-Queenie 2! Over!'

The two flying control officers are well-known professional actors, Squadron Leader Colin Tapley and Flight Lieutenant Eric Phillips. Back comes the reassuring reply. 'Q-Queenie 2 from Grateful, permission to land!' And the WAAFs in the mess who have also been listening to the radio conversation, while waiting to serve us breakfast, give a sigh of relief as another crew identifies itself. Johnny makes a perfect landing on the precious soil of England and we roll round to the dispersal. After a stretch and a cigarette we are away to the briefing room for interrogation. The intelligence officer, Section Officer Jean Johnson, has just de-briefed Squadron Leader Woollatt, Flight Commander in 12 Squadron who was the second pilot in the famous film *Target for Tonight*. Now come the questions. 'Did you see any fighters? What was the flak like? Where was it? Were the markers on time? Did you bomb the markers? Did you see any bombers go down? Where? Did you suffer any damage?' We drink mugs of rum and cocoa, dispensed by the WAAF officers who traditionally welcomed the crews back, and smoke free cigarettes – Martins, Sunripe – bundled together in wine glasses. We answer as accurately and fairly as we can, but one pilot reports that his JT gear was frozen up! More crews come in and we look at the board to see if anyone is missing. Then we are off to a meal and back to our sleeping quarters a mile and a quarter from the mess. . . .

Here on a brick by the side of my bed I make a single chalk

mark to show that the *first* of my operations has been successfully completed.

The first four of our 'ops' were to Berlin, with three flown by Johnny and one by Philip. The first raid on 18 November set fire to Albert Speer's Ministry of Armaments and War Production and he reported that his 'nearby Ministry was one gigantic conflagration'. The third of the raids was carried out in clear weather – and we learned what it was like to be caught in searchlights – and this attack not only destroyed the central telephone exchange in Berlin but also started fires in Germany's most important tank factory. Fog and low cloud meant a diversion for us to Dalton on our return and one aircraft came back so low over the North Sea that it also brought back some six feet of trawler mast embedded in the leading edge of a wing. We returned to Berlin on 16 December when the Command lost nearly thirty aircraft over Germany.

Operations were on again for us on 20 December and, as Bill Freeman and I walked into the briefing room, I observed, part in jest and part in seriousness, 'One of these days, you know, we shall find we're the only station on a target!' As we stood in front of the wall map we saw that the ribbon stretched to Mannheim. 'Good!' I exclaimed, 'especially as I'm getting married in two days' time!'

'It's not too far,' replied Bill. How many aircraft on? Forty-two! The task of the Lancaster bombers of 12 and 626 Squadrons was to draw off or confuse Germany's night fighters by a spoof attack on Mannheim while the main force of some 700 bombers went on to strike at Frankfurt. Our maximum effort from Wickenby resulted in a very accurate attack on the industry of Mannheim which left great clouds of smoke rising to 12 000 feet and more. Some battles with night fighters took place but all our aircraft came back safely. The raid on Frankfurt was a success but forty-two bombers did not come back. Our spoof on Mannheim may have split the fighter defence but it did not save the main force from considerable losses. It was, however, by this kind of deception that German fighter resources could sometimes be stretched to their limit.

My first operational leave came at Christmas. On 23 December Thelma and I were married in uniform at St Paul's, Oxgate, in north-west London. Thelma's father, who had been a sergeant in the Liverpool Regiment in the First World War and was wounded in the Battle of Cambrai, treated the wedding as a parade and my bride arrived absolutely on time. Our short honeymoon was spent in a hotel in north-west London; then it was back to Wickenby for me and Upper Heyford for Thelma.

January 1944 saw four more raids for us on Berlin and one on Brunswick. On the 20th all the 626 Squadron aircraft and crews were lined up in front of the flying control tower for a photograph before taking off for Berlin. On this raid I actually fired on a Dornier 217 from the front turret. But the photograph was banished from my mind until 1972 when, after opening Mike Garbett's and Brian Goulding's book *The Lancaster at War*, I found myself staring at this same picture, entitled *Panorama of Power* and showing the crew, with Philip and me standing together. On 27 January 'Q-Queenie 2' was struck by flak near Brandenburg and I lost a close friend on the same raid. Flight Lieutenant Noel Belford was an Australian pilot who had survived with his crew after a successful night ditching in a gale-tossed North Sea two weeks earlier. The Air Sea Rescue launches sent to pick them up had to be recalled, but a Royal Navy ML pressed on through big seas and effected a most courageous rescue by the light of flares. After two weeks' survival leave Noel went back on 'ops' and a weak radio signal suggested that he had been forced to ditch a second time; he was never seen again.

Three nights later Johnny took us to Berlin for the eighth time. On this attack Bill Breckenridge, who was in our flight, flew in 'Y-2', and, as they neared the aiming point, a fighter attacked at close range, riddling the Lanc. with cannon shells. The wireless operator was killed and the mid-upper and rear gunners seriously wounded. Bill succeeded in keeping 'Y-2' on course, but they were attacked again and the navigator was hit, but the bombing run was completed. A fighter came in again, perhaps the same one, and this time Bill was hit in the legs. A fourth attack followed and the crippled machine began to lose height. On the return over the North Sea 'Y-2' caught fire, but the mid-upper gunner and the flight engineer were able to put out the flames after a great struggle. Injured and without oxygen, Bill was still able to nurse his aircraft home to a crash landing at Docking on the Norfolk coast. He went on to complete his tour, often allowing me to come and fly his aircraft on air tests, cross-countries and other exercises; I was spending many hours at this time on pilot exercises in the link trainer. Bill Breckenridge became Air Traffic Controller at Glasgow Airport after the war and died in 1971 after a sudden illness.

Our last assault on Berlin came on 15 February. 'Q-Queenie 2' was again hit by flak, one piece missing the lower part of my body by a few inches. Forty-two bombers were lost on that mission. The Battle of Berlin had been an air operation without parallel, with a force of heavy bombers striking and often having to fight its way over 600 miles or more of enemy territory. I took part in nine of the sixteen raids that comprised that Battle. What had it achieved? What had been the cost?

The attacks on Berlin had not 'cost Germany the war' and in an operational sense we had suffered a defeat, as the scales had become more tipped in favour of the German night fighters. A total of 492 bombers had failed to return from the battle, 95 had been destroyed in crash landings and 859 had been severely damaged. The cost had also been 3500 young fliers. Yet in February 1944 Field Marshal Erhard Milch said that in his opinion Berlin could not hold out much longer. And indeed Berlin had suffered heavy damage, especially to factories, including the Siemens and Alkett works, while much of the electrical and instrument industry was forced to move from Berlin to Silesia. In twelve of the raids the loss of life had been quite small and Dr Joseph Goebbels attributed this in his Diaries to evacuation and other measures taken by the German authorities.

The Battle of Berlin was a costly climax in the whole of the air war – the end of the strategists' Bomber Dream. As the attacks went on, we saw more and more bombs being dropped over the North Sea on the way out to lessen all-up weights so that bombers and their tired crews could gain a few more feet of operational height. The losses in aircraft meant that the Command had wiped itself out and although morale suffered on a number of stations I saw no traces of it at Wickenby. We kept on going because we believed that we were contributing to victory – and Albert Speer said that if the successes against the Ruhr and Hamburg had been repeated Germany could not have survived – and we owed something as well to those who had died.

One bitter night in spite of my heated socks the tops of all my toes were frostbitten. 'Q-Queenie 2' was iced up several times and once she was illuminated by St Elmo's Fire – ghostly green flames from an electrical discharge, named after the patron saint of sailors – which danced all over the wings and the top of the fuselage.

The assault on Germany went on. We flew right down to the Swiss border, causing that neutral state to impose a rapid black-out, and crossed over a heavily defended Reich to attack the Diesel-engine works in Augsburg. The target was clear of cloud and lying in snow and was heavily bombed. In March we came back from a Frankfurt raid without reaching the target after troubles with the electrical system and the superchargers. On 23 March our faithful 'Q-Queenie 2' was borrowed by another crew and went missing, one of seventy-three bombers lost that night. One week later the Command lost ninety-seven bombers on the ill-fated raid on Nuremberg.

On 26 April Johnny Neilson took us in 'N–2' to Essen. There was no cloud above the target and it was accurately marked by the Pathfinders. It was meant to be a heavy and rapid blow on the armaments centre. The run-up to the target went off without any trouble. 'Bombs gone!' I called out, and then a most desperate shudder ran through the Lancaster. At that moment six four-pound incendiary bombs struck 'N–2'. They had been dropped, as we discovered by their angle of entry afterwards, by a Lancaster above us, which having reached the target early was flying, against orders, right into the teeth of the approaching bomber stream; his correct course would have been to orbit the target and join the stream at an angle as it moved in towards Essen.

Johnny called up all the crew members in turn. There was no response from Dick Tredwin. I went back to investigate. The mid-upper turret was completely wrecked with hydraulic fluid dripping down on to the floor. Dick, with helmet and oxygen mask off his face, was lying slumped across the breech blocks of his guns. I could not reach his head from below, as he was a well-built man. I could not tell whether he was dead or alive, but if he were the latter he would soon die without oxygen. Johnny had to bring the Lanc. down quickly over the Ruhr while we tried to extricate Dick from the wreckage. It was a struggle for us all, but he was alive, his face swollen and unrecognizable. A bomb had come through the canopy of his turret, striking him on the head, and had then wrecked the turret and passed through the floor of the aircraft, leaving a gaping hole. Another incendiary had cut its way clean through the armour-plated tricell chute which only one second before had held a photoflash with the explosive power of a 250-pound bomb. Had I delayed pressing the bomb-release button by that second the impact of the incendiary bomb would have set off the flash. As I look at the photograph which I obtained by means of that flash, the whole memory of that dreadful moment comes flooding back. The other incendiaries were lodged in the petrol tanks and had cut the main spar, leaving the rivets to take the stress of the waving wing. Fortunately none of these bombs had ignited, not having fallen far enough for the strikers to overcome their creep springs and fire the detonators.

It was a long and desperate flight back to Wickenby where ambulance and fire tenders were standing by. Johnny landed the aircraft with great skill, but its survival was a tribute to the aircraft workers of Britain. Dick had now to survive a road journey to the RAF hospital at Rauceby, as there were no medical facilities on squadrons to deal with injuries as severe as these. After a long convalescence he returned to duty. Thelma was posted up to No. 1 Group and came to Wickenby, and later Dick married the WAAF sergeant who was also on the station. He died of cancer in 1973. Flight Sergeant Rees joined us as mid-upper gunner.

The style of the air warfare began to change for us. The emphasis shifted from the strategic bombing offensive towards the needs of the forthcoming invasion of Normandy. In May I dropped a stick of fourteen high-explosive bombs across the Berliet motorworks at Venissieux near Lyons. In our new 'Q-Queenie 2' we went to France in the full moon and bombed an ammunition dump at Rennes. In early June we attacked a heavy gun battery at Sangatte in the Pas de Calais and on D-Day itself we struck at a railway junction in the Forêt de St Germain near Paris. The attack on the French railway system was to prevent the Germans bringing up armour and supplies to the beach-head. I shall never forget the sight from the air of that great armada of ships about to invade Hitler's fortress. Our night attacks continued on the centres of communication, but at Vierzonville we met strong fighter opposition. On a trip to Dijon the compasses began to precess and I was forced to map-read from St Malo to the target and back. By this time Philip had been promoted to Group Captain and after a short spell at Sandtoft had become the Station Commander at Wickenby. In June we in Bomber Command had a new experience – precision raids in daylight. It began with an attack by 234 Lancasters and Mosquitoes just before sunset on the harbour and E-boat pens at Le Havre. In 1973 I stood on the spot in Le Havre where my first bomb had landed. Nearly every ship was sunk at Le Havre, including a fleet of light naval vessels and, with a complementary attack on Boulogne, more than a hundred E-boats were destroyed in the two ports.

On our return from Aulnoye in the middle of June with Philip Haynes we had been overtaken by a small fast aircraft with a tail light which passed over the Sussex coast in a hail of tracer bullets and crashed near Petworth in a great sheet of flame. It was, of course, a V 1 – a flying bomb – of which we in the Command had received advance warning. Later Thelma and I experienced the V 1 blitz in London and found it very unpleasant. In June we went with Johnny, having been briefed to be the last of some 240 Lancasters detailed to attack a flying-bomb site at Les Hayons to the south-east of Dieppe. My task was to bomb the site with high explosives and to take a 60 per cent line overlap photograph of the attack as the last aircraft to bomb and so produce a record of the raid's success.

In London the V 2s were soon to follow the V 1s. After the first rocket fell in London a rumour spread that Chiswick gasworks had blown up. Some mornings later a vibrant explosion and the ensuing death-rattle of a second rocket brought my mother-in-law on to the landing in her nightdress exclaiming, 'Surely it can't be another gasworks!' Thelma and I, who were on leave, knew the truth.

To prepare the way for an offensive at Caen in Normandy and at the request of 21st Army Group a force of more than 200 Lancasters was despatched on the evening of 7 July to attack German troop and armour concentrations. The fighting around the old historic city had become bogged down in stalemate and this was an attempt to get the British and Canadians on the move once more. We ran in over the Normandy beach-head. It was a clear summer evening and the air was full of Lancasters and hundreds of bursting flak shells, each leaving a round black cloud. Two Lancs in front of us flew steadily on, committed to their bombing runs and timed flights, converging slowly and with dreadful inevitability until they collided. Pieces of engine cowling flew past us and bits of wreckage struck the leading edges of our wings. One aircraft lost height and disappeared below us; the other flew on. 2350 tons of high explosive fell on the target in just over half an hour. Field Marshal Montgomery reported that 'it was a most inspiring sight to see the might of Bomber Command arriving to join in the battle', and he sent a message of congratulation to Sir Arthur Harris. On our return to Wickenby there was also a telegram from General Sir Miles Dempsey, Commander of the 2nd Army. Unfortunately the ground attack afterwards was delayed until the next morning and the Germans were given time to recover. The advancing Allies also ran into a difficult, cratered terrain, but after two days of fighting the city fell. This was Johnny Neilson's last operation.

My last operation came on 18 July when Philip Haynes took us on another daylight raid in the area of Caen. Take-off was 0417 hours and we flew south to bomb German positions near Sannerville to the south-east of the wrecked city. This was a prelude to the massive 'Goodwood' offensive, timed for the same day, which began with high promise but quickly ground to a halt. It was a strange flight home – my last operational mission in Europe – back to England and a second tour of 'ops', I supposed, against the Japanese. We shook hands on landing and said very little. There was nothing much to say. Philip invited me to have breakfast with him in his quarters, then I left to add the last chalk mark on my bedroom wall. Philip went on to tour the world, becoming Air Attaché in Washington and Air Liaison Officer in South Africa. He left the RAF in 1958 and is now Managing Director of Matra (UK) Ltd which supplies the service with modern weapons. He also married a WAAF Code and Cypher officer, Paddy Clark, who had been at my engagement party at Upper Heyford, and whom I had introduced to Philip.

After being posted as an instructor to Sandtoft in the Isle of Axholme I took a Bombing Leaders' course at Manby which won me a selection board and a post at the new Bomber Command Instructors' School at Finningley. I was promoted to flight lieutenant and I also learned that I had been awarded the D.F.C. Thelma was stationed for a time at No. 100 Squadron at Waltham near Grimsby, where we became very friendly with the dental officer at Waltham, Flight Lieutenant George Burton, and his delightful wife Joan, who lived in a caravan, owned a boat on the Humber, a Jaguar and a giant St Bernard, and displayed commendable optimism throughout the war. On VE-Day George and I succeeded in scaling the camp water tower – no mean feat with its domed, unladdered summit – but champagne and pre-war beer, released for just this occasion, fortified us for the task. George and Joan are among our best-loved friends.

Shortly after VE-Day, flanked by Air Marshal Sir Roderic Hill of Fighter Command and Air Chief Marshal Sir Arthur Longmore, I proudly took the salute at a vast victory rally of the Air Training Corps in Hyde Park. Thelma and I then went to Penzance for our second honeymoon and were rewarded with sun, blue sea and a welter of wild flowers. We walked the cliffs at Lamorna and we met Miss Rowena Cade by the granite amphitheatre on her land at Porthcurno which is now the Minack Theatre. What a contrast all this was to the grey flatness of Lincolnshire and the roar of warplanes! We visited Harry Rountree in his studio at Porthmeor Sands near St Ives. Famous for his Mansion Polish mice, he was also – although this is not so well-known – a fine painter of wild birds. He was the father of Section Officer Lynda Rountree at Upper Heyford, one of Thelma's closest friends.

In August the atomic bombs were dropped on Japan and I listened over my radio in the Officers' Mess at Finningley to the Prime Minister, Clement Attlee, announcing the end of the war. On hearing the news, Thelma, who had just been demobbed, set off for London and we celebrated VJ-Day together. For the last five months of my RAF career at Finningley we found lodgings in Bawtry village with a miner and his family. In September 1945 the AOC-in-C, Bomber Command, Sir Arthur Harris, was succeeded by Air Chief Marshal Sir Norman Bottomley. Shortly afterwards I had the pleasure of conducting him round my part of the section at BCIS. A calm and meticulous man, he later became Director of Administration at the BBC, where I met him again. In January 1946 I applied for a Class B release; I wanted to go back to Oxford and start on a Diploma in Education course, so that I could embark on a new life as a schoolmaster. For me the war was over, but the experiences and memories would remain. In fact, those wartime years often seem closer to me than many that came later.

55 573 British and Commonwealth airmen died in Bomber Command and 8325 aircraft were lost. After the war controversy and recrimination were to sully the memory of those who died. But the actions of wartime must be judged in the context of the period. In January 1944 I wrote at Wickenby how:

> Friends can die, as if in the routine of a day,
> Some quietly, unobserved, and others in the cataclysm.

I had been very fortunate and for me each day since the war has been a kind of bonus – a gift to be treasured and not frittered away.

9
Pedagogy

It was no use! I sat and wrote, looked again at the paper in front of me and tore it up. My problem was to write my first essay for nearly five years and the task was almost beyond me. Thelma and I were now living in a top-floor flat, recently vacated by my parents, who, having left Appleby, had come to Oxford for a spell before finally moving on to my brother Thomas's cottage in the Northamptonshire village of Badby. The flat was an eyrie in a large North Oxford villa in Polstead Road belonging to my aunt and uncle, Dora and Frank Fox.

The Diploma course was stimulating and I enjoyed the lectures by my tutor, C. H. Dobinson, and Dr B. A. Yeaxlee the Reader in Educational Psychology. Oxford in 1946 was a mixture of pink-faced schoolboys and undergraduates and postgraduates returning from the war, strangely clad in dufflecoats, greatcoats and combat jackets.

Gradually I began to pick up the threads of living once more. Old friends had returned – Frank Bonsall from the Royal Engineers, Douglas Grant from the Commandos, Arthur Jacobs from the Royal Artillery and Philip Stibbe from the Chindits. Donald Rawcliffe did not come back; he had died of wounds in the Middle East in July 1942. College life was austere and there was an atmosphere of seriousness and industry.

1946 was very much a year of change. My eldest brother Thomas began his new career of training teachers at the City of Coventry Training College; he was later to join the staff at Homerton College in Cambridge where he remained until his retirement in 1974. Wilfrid was appointed to the headship of Cheadle Grammar School that same year; five years later he became headmaster of Stratford Grammar School and in 1959 of Penistone. Margaret's husband, Deryck Winterton, returned to journalism and later became the chief leader writer of the *Daily Mirror*. In September 1946 I went to carry out my term's teaching practice at the Hugh Clopton School (now Stratford High) – a new and spacious Warwickshire secondary modern school under the headship of George Darlow. I was soon eased by him into full-time teaching so that I was able to take part in the full life of the school. The new Education Act that came into force in April 1945 was borne on the high hopes that it would bring about a 'new deal' in English education. The task of the secondary modern school was conceived in terms of livelihood, leisure and citizenship with opportunities for experiment and a better understanding of pupils and their needs. It was to founder on parental demands for certificates and bits of paper.

After declining an invitation to teach at the Alliance High School in Kenya I went instead to a secondary modern in Rugby. Hampered by old buildings and teaching ideas, it was not possible to develop 'the new Jerusalem' here and I moved with relief to another school in the authority.

Thelma and I rented a top flat in a tall Victorian terrace in the Bilton Road, not far from the centre of Rugby and Lawrence Sheriff School where Thomas had taught for a number of years. We acquired a mongrel pup, Crackers, whose mother belonged to Thomas. The summer of 1947 was a very long and hot one, bringing clouded yellow butterflies to the Midlands and hummingbird hawk-moths to our Rugby bedroom and to my parents' garden at Badby. I joined the West Midland Bird Club and started a school natural history society. I also spent many happy hours censusing the birds in a fine oakwood at Badby where the dawn choruses among the tall trees and the bluebell glades were some of the richest that I have ever heard. Later I was to describe this wood in some detail in a New Naturalist volume that I wrote for Collins on woodland birds.

During the long hot summer we played a lot of tennis and met a young Dutchman, Franz Wildeboer, who also joined the Rugby Lawn Tennis Club. He was training as a pilot with the RAF at Church Lawford, just outside the town. This shy and diffident young man was a frequent guest of ours in Bilton Road. As an active teenage member of the Dutch underground

Pedagogy

he had graduated from blowing up troop trains to preparing and distributing copies of the multitude of passes and official forms used by the German authorities. He had crossed occupied Europe, holding a dual identity, to recover members of the underground from camps in Czechoslovakia and he had survived interrogation by the Gestapo. After he had been awarded his pilot's wings he invited us to have a fortnight's holiday with him in Holland. His parents and sister lived in a large detached house in Aerdenhout near Haarlem, still wired with anti-German warning devices.

My first visit to that great bird reserve – the Naardermeer – was a tremendous experience. Franz introduced me to the famous Dutch bird photographer, J. P. Strijbos, and through his good offices I was able to get a permit to spend a whole day on the reserve with a local boatman. We conversed by signs and sketches in my field notebook and in this way we talked about such interesting topics as his children, his work for the underground and the current bakers' strike in Amsterdam. For the birds I used Coward's *Birds of the British Isles*, as this was before the era of the field guides. There are nearly two thousand acres of reeds and waterways on the Naardermeer. Here we slowly drifted or paddled our way across the pools and along remote channels where the tall reeds nearly shut out the sky. Two marsh harriers and three Montagu's flapped along close to the boat. Both reed and great reed warblers churred and chattered away among the tall stems while I could see great crested grebes, teal, mallard, shoveler, garganey and red-crested pochards floating quietly on the small secluded lakes. I was particularly thrilled to see eight spoonbills and seven purple herons – two species which once had a wide European distribution. There were also about a thousand cormorants – white-headed birds of the Continental race – and small numbers of black terns, redshanks and common sandpipers. It was a day of total separation from urban living and one of the best in my life.

In Rugby we became very friendly with a teaching colleague, Peter Everard, who had been taught by Thomas in Rugby. Like us he was ex-RAF and with other willing helpers we set up a new branch of the Royal Air Forces Association. It was opened by our President, Air Commodore Sir Frank Whittle, who in the 1930s had battled against Air Ministry scepticism to establish the jet engine which, with later Ministry backing, was to be developed near Rugby and would revolutionize the RAF and bring a new look to civil aviation. He had just been awarded £100 000 tax free for his work and had immediately been plagued by begging letters from 'mad inventors and a lot of people who were mad, but not inventors. If people had written "Can you spare a dime, pal?" I would not have minded, but no one asked for less than £50. One man said he really needed £5000 but would be quite happy to receive only £500!'

In the summer of 1948 I was appointed to the staff of the school in Stratford where I had carried out my teaching-practice term. Here I took over the English department and was given great scope to develop project teaching in the school. I also produced the school play, Leopold Lewis's *The Bells*, admirably designed by William Lofthouse, who was the art master. It was difficult to find somewhere to live near Stratford-upon-Avon and we ended up by renting two rooms, one up and one down, in a large farmhouse near Preston-on-Stour. The setting was delightful, with Meon Hill – the first bastion of the Cotswolds – visible from our bedroom window.

I joined the Alscot Park Cricket Club and with regular matches against Stratford, Rugby, Leamington, Banbury and Southam I enjoyed a high standard of cricket. Our home ground, on which I found fast bowling a true pleasure, was set amongst tall elms and grazing fallow deer. Thelma became the official scorer and we had many delightful visits for our away matches. One summer's day I was fielding at first slip on the ground at Ragley Hall – the magnificent home of the Marquess of Hertford with its parklands originally designed by Capability Brown. The wicket was easy-paced and runs were coming slowly. Three wickets had fallen when a fleet of black bombers flying low over the field shattered the calm and put a stop to the game. It was then resumed, only to be interrupted once more as a large bough from an ancient oak crashed down on the ladies' lavatory, fortunately unoccupied at the time. A second branch fell and when a swarm of bees bore down on us in a humming black cloud and passed between the wickets at a height of only six feet, hotly pursued by mid-on, several of the players were on the verge of hysteria!

I went bird-watching with a new intensity, often joining up with C. A. (Tony) Norris who lived in Stratford-upon-Avon and had organized the nation-wide corncrake enquiry. We visited the Midland reservoirs and lakes to look for wildfowl and wading birds, went batfowling at night along the drive of the Welcombe Hotel, catching and ringing finches, and explored local starling roosts. In November 1949 Peter Cairns and recording engineer Stanley Unwin from the BBC in Birmingham visited my local starling roost for their radio programme to find out how we caught and marked birds. I discovered a visible migration route for birds across the farm; it could be traced back to Rugby in one direction and to Cheltenham in the other. I called this flyway 'the Cotswold corridor'. My observations were written up in a paper for the journal *British Birds* and later formed the basis of my book *Bird Migrants* which was published in 1952. I was invited to join the Research Committee of the West Midland Bird Club and I was appointed by the Chief Constable of Warwickshire, Lt.-Colonel G. C. White, and sworn in as the first special constable with responsibility for bird protection.

Life in Stratford was very full. I particularly enjoyed the lectures I gave for the Extra-Mural Department of Birmingham University, both in Edmund Street and during the residential weekend courses at the adult education college at Westham House, near Barford, run by the admirable Captain Frank Owen. The 390th meeting of the Shakespeare Club at Mason Croft was devoted to the birds of Shakespeare. I talked about many of the forty-three different kinds of birds that were well known to the bard. Stratford also had a very vigorous debating society called the Wranglers and I can remember one meeting when I opposed Kenneth Griffith, the actor and film director, on the motion that 'human welfare owed more to science than the poetic imagination'. The motion was carried by one vote, 75–74, with almost fifty abstentions.

During two summers Thelma and I went to stay with her sister Jeanne and her husband Lewis Gordon in the fishing port of Peterhead – a somewhat forbidding rose-red granite town on the coast of Aberdeenshire. I learned to love the wide-open spaces of Buchan, with its enormous skies and rolling plateau of green pastures and heather-brown moors which fell 200 feet into the North Sea. Here each bit of coast had its special charm – Longhaven where the sea has eaten a great gully out of the granite; the Bullers o'Buchan where an enormous circular cavern can be entered through an archway from the sea and remote Slains Castle where the Two Eyes – 'the Twa Een' – look out across the rocky bay. In summer the cliffs are soft with rushes and grass while clumps of thrift, clusters of scurvy grass and fleshy roseroot clothe their faces. Herring gulls nest on the cliff-tops and the stacks, while gentle-looking kittiwakes hang their seaweed nests on tiny shelves above the breaking waves. Guillemots pack along the ledges and razorbills find cracks and crevices for their homes. Puffins, now very uncommon, excavate holes in the turf and fulmars float past with consummate ease and scarcely a wingbeat. Shags have untidy nests on the lower rocks and in the sea caverns. Starlings and house sparrows feed their young in deep rock cracks, and house martins, with all the wisdom of their ancestors, build their mud cups in caves and chimneys where the rock doves have their secret hide-outs. Eider ducks bob on the water among great rafts of ducks and gulls, oystercatchers pipe on some of the wave-washed boulders, and from time to time a rock pipit goes up to parachute down singing his high repetitive song. For me it provided much-needed spiritual refreshment and the oil barons had not yet moved in.

In 1948 I went out for a sixteen-hour voyage on the Peterhead drifter *Expert* under an experienced skipper, James Strachan. With their tall funnels smoking, 126 boats sailed in the afternoon out of Peterhead inner harbour and past the giant granite mole still being built by convict labour from the nearby prison. It was an impressive and wonderful sight. I never saw it quite like this again, as the fishing industry soon began to decline. For five hours we pushed east into a choppy sea and the drifter pitched and rolled alarmingly. I stayed up on deck watching the fulmars and gulls flying round the boat. A sudden shout called me below for tea and I clambered down into an atmosphere of hot oil, paraffin, cigarette smoke and ancient fish. A plate full of fatty lumps of fried bacon was put before me and this had to be washed down with huge cups of tea half-filled with condensed milk.

The nets were shot in the dark and then, with her engine cut, the *Expert* slopped and rolled about with no forward motion and I had to readjust to this new sensation. In the dark early hours of the morning the nets were hauled in by hand – a long and arduous task. The herrings now began to drop out of the net – beautiful in a glowing warm pink and steely blue but losing their colour as they died. Gulls wailed in the dark and some of the bolder ones pulled fish out of the net as it broke the surface of the water. At last the catch was in! It was a good one and I proved no Jonah!

My headmaster bought a large house in Welford-on-Avon and invited us to share half with him. So we left Preston Pastures and moved into Newington House. There was a paddock where barn owls hunted, a large garden with fine walnut trees, acacias, a riot of old-fashioned roses and lawns that took a lot of cutting. At that time it was a delightful spot looking towards the Cotswolds and the village green with its maypole where schoolchildren on May morning danced and twined their ribbons. Not far away was the Avon, where in summer a near horizon of low wooded hills was set around the wild garden of the river-banks.

I was enjoying the pedagogic life in Stratford. I found it demanding but most rewarding. Art master Bill Lofthouse and I regularly visited the camp at Long Marston to teach displaced Poles English. There was a stimulating cultural life in the town and, of course, there was 'The Theatre'. We had Shakespeare in the summer and we could enjoy try-outs in the winter. In this way we saw Alec Clunes and Richard Burton in *The Lady's Not for Burning* and Paul Scofield in *Alexander the Great*. Ruth Draper came and gave us one of her incredible solo entertainments. We formed many friendships and our very close friends, George and Joan Burton, were now living in Handsworth Wood in Birmingham where George had established a flourishing practice. Life had taken on a straightforward pattern and the future seemed settled. But, of course, life is not like that.

10

Stalking Wildlife with a Microphone

One morning in September 1950 I received a letter from my brother-in-law Deryck Winterton. I read it on top of the bus taking me into Stratford-upon-Avon for my day's teaching. It began: 'I wondered whether you might be interested in the enclosed advert from the *Manchester Guardian* of Sept. 13th.' The small cutting reported that the BBC was inviting applications for the post of Assistant in Central Programmes Operations Department 'to make sound recordings in the whole field of natural history and to write scripts and produce programmes introducing such recordings'. When the letter arrived at Welford there were only twenty-four hours to go before the closing date was up. So, in front of my first class of the day, who had been admonished to read silently and 'Woe betide any boy who took his eyes off the book!', I wrote out my formal application for this exciting post. Many weeks were to go by before I heard that I had been short-listed and many months before I learned that nearly 500 other applications had been received by the BBC.

The appointments board met on 9 November. Its chairman was R. H. J. Gillet and its members included F. L. Hetley, Bruce Campbell of the British Trust for Ornithology, and R. V. A. George – better known as Brian, who as Head of Central Programmes Operations was for the next seven years to be my colleague, friend and champion in the Corporation. He gave me independence and a trust which allowed me to carry out my experimental work with complete freedom. He was to die tragically in 1969 after an accident on the day before his retirement was due to take place. After the board I had to read a script over a closed circuit. Not until the next day, when I saw an article by Robert Cannell in the *Daily Express,* did I know that the post for which I had applied had arisen through the BBC's decision not to renew Dr Ludwig Koch's contract.

On 18 December the Corporation announced that I had been appointed as resident ornithologist to succeed Dr Koch, the Frankfurt-born director of a German record manufacturing company who had come to Britain in 1936 as a refugee from Nazi oppression. Violinist, lieder-singer and pioneer of bird recording Ludwig Koch had made in 1889 the historic first recording of a bird's voice – that of a caged white-rumped or common shama. With the assistance of Sir Julian Huxley, H. F. Witherby and E. M. Nicholson, who introduced him to ornithologists, birds and locations, he built up on discs what is now the historic core of the natural history section of the BBC's Sound Archives. Ludwig greatly deplored his retirement from the BBC and that he was not allowed 'to train a new man', but in this respect the Corporation showed considerable foresight. On my appointment he sent out, as one newspaper correspondent aptly put it, 'alarm calls to the Press with the emotional spontaneity of an angry blackbird'. This remarkable and durable man was to live to the age of ninety-two.

After my appointment I went on living at Welford and daily travelled to the BBC's Engineering School at Wood Norton near Evesham only a few miles away. Here I came to grips with the theory of recording on disk, wire, film and tape, brushing up my school certificate physics as I went along. I learned to line up a recording channel for use and ran out cables to microphone positions in the woods and copses at Wood Norton. I cut disks carrying bird calls and songs and the first wildlife recording that I ever made in the field was of the spring song of a robin in the winter of 1950–1. It is now in the BBC's Sound Archives.

I was most anxious to try out tape for the first time and in the spring of 1951 I arranged an experiment in Kensington Gardens whereby the dawn bird songs near the statue of Peter Pan would be recorded simultaneously on both the old portable disk recorder, which the BBC used for outside work, and a new tape apparatus. The output of the same microphone was to be used to keep a constant level on the most powerful singer. When I listened to the results of the Peter Pan experiment in a studio in Broadcasting House there was less surface noise audible on the tape and more birds could be heard which gave the tape recording a natural depth and perspective. Another advantage lay in the higher recording time possible with tape.

Once I was satisfied that tape was the answer to wildlife recording I began to plan my projects for the year ahead. Timothy Eckersley, the son of the former BBC planner, Roger Eckersley, and a great grandson of T. H. Huxley, was responsible for the processing of material for the Sound Archives and he suggested that I should listen to all the natural history recordings to discover the gaps and make a note of older ones that could be replaced. I also investigated new material that had been collected by Sture Palmér, the great Swedish bird recordist. For some time it proved impossible to arrange a meeting with Ludwig Koch, but it was finally achieved. He found it difficult to accept that I had started making recordings and his wife Nellie exclaimed on first meeting me, 'But you are so young!'

'Time', I said, 'will cure that!'

In the spring of 1951 I approached John Parrinder, who had made a special study of the little ringed plover. I needed his help in recording this rather rare breeding bird, one of whose haunts was about to be flooded for ever. I have always required very special reasons for recording any rare bird in Britain. The site was the unfinished William Girling reservoir in Essex. After making several recces of the area – and this, in my opinion, is a vital bit of activity for all sound recordists – I came back in June with a friend of my Stratford days, BBC recording engineer Stanley Unwin, better known today as 'Professor' Stanley Unwin, master of the double-talk act on radio and television and a star of the film *Chitty-Chitty-Bang-Bang*. We had with us a new tape recorder in two separate units operated from a twelve-volt battery. We parked the recording car on the concrete wall of the reservoir and from it I ran out 300 yards of cable to a nest that John Parrinder had found. I dug a hole in the loose gravel two feet from the nest and covered all but the face of the microphone with stones. In less than four minutes I was clambering up the wall again and, as I turned back, I saw the hen bird through my binoculars running back to the nest to settle on her eggs once more. We recorded many conversational calls in this way; some were very quiet and were only audible with the unaided ear a few feet away. In June Eric Hosking and George Edwards came to take photographs of the pair on whose nest and lives we were so busily eavesdropping.

Not far from this nest another little ringed plover was calling anxiously and trying to marshal some tiny downy chicks. As they were always on the move, a fixed microphone was quite useless and a different technique was needed. I believe that I was the first to use a parabolic reflector for wildlife recording in Britain. The principle itself is quite simple. Sound waves strike the curved surface of the reflector's bowl or dish and are then reflected to a focal point just in front, where a dynamic microphone is fixed facing into the bowl and with its back to the sound. The device increases the pick-up of sounds coming from the direction in which the reflector is sighted. It needs to be used with discretion in open situations and not close to reflecting surfaces such as walls, houses and cliffs. As long ago as 1953 I wrote in *British Birds* about reflectors – 'At all times their limitations must be realized for full value to be derived from them.' To dismiss them as some sound recordists have done is to deny oneself the aid of a valuable device. During the Kensington Gardens tape experiment I had used a reflector with a three-foot diameter and I went on to record fieldfares in the Midlands at 200 yards' range and a cuckoo in Kent at 420 yards. For the little ringed plovers I relied on a less obvious reflector only eighteen inches across which was lighter and more easily moved about. The big reflector needed a camera tripod to support it.

Ludwig Koch came to see me in my office on the fifth floor of Broadcasting House and I asked him, 'Would you like to hear my new recordings of the little ringed plover?'

'You mean, zee ringed plovva?' he answered.

'No,' I repeated the phrase, 'the *little* ringed plover.'

'But zat iss a verra rare borrd!'

I had received the accolade from the master! I saw him many

times after that and broadcast with him in several programmes. I recall with especial delight a programme called *Masterpieces of Bird Recording* in which he and I were joined by John Kirby, E. D H. Johnson and Roger Perry; the programme, broadcast in May 1960, was presented by the late James Fisher and produced by Jeffrey Boswall.

In June John McMillan, then Assistant Controller of the Light Programme, asked me to devise a programme about the dawn chorus and this provided me with an opportunity for a unique experiment in broadcasting. Eight BBC mobile recording engineers and their units with eight ornithologists recorded and documented the dawn chorus on the same morning in different parts of Britain. I am quite sure that the Corporation's mobile units were never again called out in such strength so early, but the experiment, called *Heralds of the Dawn*, was a great success. In that same summer a rather unusual quiz was held between England and Scotland – an international bird-song contest with Percy Edwards – the bird mimic – as referee. Brian Johnston opened the programme from London while the Hon. Henry Douglas-Home, who had introduced live bird-song broadcasts from a Surrey wood in the 1930s, and Douglas Fleming presented alternate three-minute transmissions of songs; these Percy identified and gave marks to with extra points for rarity. The microphone positions were very critical and on one occasion Henry had had to move a courting couple who parked themselves under his key microphone only minutes before the programme went on the air!

I was invited to stay as a guest at the Hirsel with the Earl and Countess of Home to watch the Scottish contribution to the quiz go on the air. Henry in dew-soaked tennis shoes gave me a conducted tour of the estate where we saw three pairs of turtle doves in what was then their only Scottish breeding station. With the help of nest-boxes Henry greatly increased the breeding population of pied flycatchers and his swift boxes were to capture the interest of Prince Philip during a visit that he paid to the Hirsel. The Earl died not long after my stay in his vast and elegant eighteenth-century home, but Thelma and I stayed later with Lilian, the Dowager Countess. The air of delightful informality and the relaxed and humorous conversation made our visits particularly enjoyable.

In October 1951, while I was in Berwickshire, I joined Sir Peter Scott at Greenlaw to make recordings of pink-footed geese which were being caught in rocket-propelled nets for ringing, examination and tail dipping in purple dye for easier recognition. The wind was rather high and the results were not as good as I would have liked. In October 1955 I went on another rocket-netting expedition with Peter and in Kinross I was able to collect recordings of small flocks of geese, massed flights and the rocket-net being fired over the geese. I had now started seriously to collect winter recordings. These included redwings and fieldfares, rooks and jackdaws and white-fronted geese. From the lake in Holkham Park in Norfolk, where Lord Leicester gave me permission to work and in return for which I catalogued his bird collection, recordings were obtained of Canada and Egyptian geese and some of my favourite sounds – the down-slurred whistles of drake wigeon and the rolling calls of the ducks. I met Dick Bagnall-Oakeley at a meeting of the London Natural History Society – the start of a long and rewarding friendship – and he invited me to see and record a black-bellied dipper at Aylsham while recordings of tawny owls, duck and fenland atmospheres were also made on Wheatfen Broad which belonged to E. A. (Ted) Ellis – a fine all-round field naturalist.

About this time a 'midget' tape recorder was evolved that weighed less than twenty pounds and was completely self-contained. In March 1952 I took one of these tape machines at low tide from Hilbre Island in the Cheshire Dee to nearby Middle Hilbre. I was introduced to these remarkable bird-islands by Norman Ellison – 'Nomad' of the BBC's North Region – and William (Bill) Wilson. They invited me to join what was called the 'Hilbre Group' whose members included not only themselves, but Field Marshal Lord Alanbrooke, Eric Hosking, Roger Tory Peterson, John Parrinder, Dr Grant McAfee, Joe Wells, Ronald Pryor and John Craggs. Later its most illustrious member was to be Prince Philip. When I joined the party with its camaraderie, good humour and shared chores I knew that I was going to enjoy myself. I had borrowed one of Eric Hosking's hides and I put it up near some rocks at the northern end of Middle Hilbre. A great deal of photographic work had been done over the years on the islands but this was the first attempt to make sound recordings. I put the microphone some ten feet from the hide and retired inside it. Slowly and inexorably the waters of the Dee moved up the island shore. From my peephole in the hide I could see hundreds of knot banking and twisting, driven from the estuary and its sandbanks by the rising tide. Suddenly flocks of grey birds began to cascade down from the sky and in a few minutes 4000 birds were landing and jostling each other for a foothold only forty feet away. Swiftly the ledge of rock where the hide was perched began to disappear under a living carpet of birds. I recorded tape after tape, but as the tide finally ebbed the birds began to depart.

About this time I suggested to the BBC that, although I would continue to obtain some recordings myself, it would be helpful to have a second and regular member of the team – a recording engineer who would accompany me on all the major trips, supervise gear, try out new experiments and maintain with me a continuity of experience. The successful applicant was G. F. (Bob) Wade – a forthright, outspoken character of great professional skill who had joined the BBC in 1941. He had accompanied Richard Dimbleby on bomber operations and the airborne crossing of the Rhine, and had also preserved for posterity the German surrender to Field Marshal Montgomery at Lüneburg Heath and the long Nuremberg war trials. With his experience, which included several royal tours, a keen interest in fishing and the open air, he proved to be a stalwart and reliable colleague.

My favourite British wild mammal is the badger, with his independence, clean habits and retiring nature. For me he represented a great challenge. Apart from a brief snatch of sound obtained by Oliver Pike there was no material available for study and very little was known about the animal's language. In May 1951 Maxwell Knight came to see me in Broadcasting House and so began a close friendship which lasted until his death in 1968. A man of many talents – broadcaster, lecturer, authority on traditional jazz, writer, and all-round naturalist, Max had infinite warmth and humanity. He introduced me to a magnificent badger sett in the middle of a Theosophist community in Surrey where the animals were tame enough to accept buns thrown at them and to climb dustbins in order to knock off the lids of others close by. I first visited the sett on a warm July afternoon and found that the entrances were grouped around a large central mound, surrounded by pines, oaks and cedars and huge clumps of rhododendrons. Bob and I came back to set up microphones around the sett. We conditioned our badgers to come and eat what we put out for them at spots under the microphones. Here we were to work for over four years. Gradually we collected the various calls – the grunts, warning calls, threats, purrs, yarls, screams, play noises, fights between sows and the gosling-like calls of tiny cubs. So well had Bob and I conditioned the badgers with the help of local residents that in April 1953 Ernest Neal – the world authority on the badger – and Professor Humphrey Hewer came to make a cine film at night of our special animals. In the end I collected thirteen separate calls and a full account of the badger project was published in my book *Voices of the Wild*.

There were many interesting places that I visited in my quest for wildlife recordings. I made a score of visits to Minsmere on the Suffolk coast – a reserve of the Royal Society for the Protection of Birds largely created by flooding in 1940 as a defence against Hitler's tanks. Here we recorded all the calls of a pair of stone curlews – handsome and rare waders of stony ground – from their first arrival in Suffolk in early April until the young birds left the nest. These included the frenzied nuptial displays, the loud clear whistles of territorial ownership, the alarms and the typical 'coo-ee' flight call. After we had located the nest I put an open microphone close to it and covered it with pieces of turf. In this way we were able to capture the low calls of the adults just as I had done in the previous year with the little ringed plovers. Just after ten o'clock one fine May morning we listened with growing excitement to very faint cheeps coming from inside one of the shells, which we checked was still unbroken. The hen with low clucking notes encouraged the little bird to make that first big effort to crack the shell from inside with its egg tooth. Curiously enough, on the same date and in the same temperature a pair of stone curlews, being watched by Commander A. W. P. Robertson fifty miles away, left the chipping egg alone for up to 105 minutes. All the stone curlew recordings can be heard on a BBC Records disk on East Anglia in the Wildlife Series.

From Minsmere Bob and I reaped a rich harvest of recordings – the calls and boom of bitterns, notes of bearded tits, little grebes, garganey and reed warblers in the reedbeds, of redshank, spotted redshank, shelduck and little terns on the mudflats, of songbirds in the woodlands and on the heaths. In April 1964, when I was directing a film about the wildlife at Minsmere, I was able to record on my portable tape machine the very rare spring display of the male marsh harrier given in a special flight several hundred feet up in the air. And in subsequent years I added the calls of water pipit and kingfisher and the sound of thousands of starlings performing their aerial manoeuvres before going to roost in the reed beds.

One of my great friends was Alec, the Commander Robertson who had also been studying stone curlews. We spent many days in the field together in Breckland, whose sandy steppe-like countryside lies between the three towns of Swaffham, Newmarket and Bury St Edmunds. Formerly a House Officer at the Royal Naval College at Dartmouth and Comptroller to HRH the Duke of Gloucester, Alec was invalided out of the Royal Navy in 1949 and devoted his newly acquired leisure to conservation and photographing birds. For twenty-five years he had also studied the crossbills of Breckland and since these rare birds were continually harassed by egg collectors we carried on our telephone conversations about them in code. In March 1953 Bob and I made a special trip to record the vocabulary of this bird. It was a very successful expedition, crowned with a recording of the bird's rarely given full song; in twenty-one years Alec Robertson had only heard it twice. Alec and I also served together on the Council of the RSPB. His death in 1956 was a very sad blow and an appreciation by another bird photographer, George Yeates, in the society's magazine *Bird Notes* recalled his great qualities: '. . . he was a gay, charming and intelligent gentleman. Above all, in every respect he was in truth a very dear person.'

For the birds of the tidal mudflats and saltmarshes I made many trips to Cley on the North Norfolk coast, since it had been highly praised to me by another outstanding bird photographer, Dick Bagnall-Oakeley. Once 'Cley-next-the-Sea', it is now more strictly 'Cley-One-Mile-from-the-Sea'. Our base was usually the George where Mrs Eve Burnett, a most vivacious and attractive personality, was the hostess. She made us delightfully at home, allowing us to get up at any time of the night or day to make coffee, prepare breakfast or boil up mussels in white wine in her kitchen. In those days it was a real bird-watchers' hotel and Eve Burnett was quite conditioned to seeing her dining-room suddenly empty after a face had appeared in the doorway to announce 'There's a red-breasted flycatcher up at the Point!' or 'There's a red-necked phalarope by the East Bank!' We concentrated on making recordings of migrant waders such as greenshank, dunlin, wood sandpiper and grey plover, as well as gulls, ducks and Brent geese. One bitter February day our little folding boat *Puffin* carried us and our gear across Blakeney Sound into the teeth of an Arctic gale. Conditions were so bad that we had only gone because a Cley fisherman-friend Stanley Webster promised to keep an eye open on the weather in case it should deteriorate further. As our Seagull outboard motor chugged us forward, parties of goldeneye rose and wheeled overhead, the drakes flashing white bellies and wing squares. Thirty shore larks were feeding on the nearby shingle ridge and 150 snow buntings were being tossed about like snowflakes in the north-west wind. On the far side we hauled the *Puffin* across 200 yards of oozy tidal mudflat towards some sheltering belts of suaeda and marram grass. We were making for a tiny wooden hut on the Hood near Blakeney Point which was to be our shelter for several days.

The wind now shifted to the north-east and, as the tide ebbed amongst the snow flurries, birds began to collect on the mudflats – a mass of grey knot, mixed parties of curlew and bar-tailed godwits, turnstone, dunlin and a single purple sandpiper. Four grey plover from the Arctic tundra flew past the hut. As the tide ebbed further, leaving a wide fringe of ice along the shore, Brent geese and shelducks began to alight and dibble in the Sound. Across the freezing grey mud came the laughing notes of the ducks and the coarse rolling 'rrook-rrooks' of the Brents. It was so cold in the hut that I sat with a paraffin stove between my legs, then went out to stump around for a while, leaving the heater for Bob. In the middle of our last night a dramatic and terrifying combination of gale and tide produced a mountain of water that pounded the hut on all sides. On this great tide, which was punching huge breaches in the shingle ridge, and in a blinding blizzard we set out in the little boat for Cley and shelter.

For me the Highlands of Scotland have always proved an irresistible magnet. My first recording expedition was in 1953 and Bob and I made our base in a disused boathouse near Loch Morlich. We hauled 1200 feet of plastic cable up a cliff face to record the stirring sounds of peregrines and their eyasses, and several days were spent recording the lovely voices of Highland wading birds – snipe, ringed plover, oystercatchers, common sandpipers and greenshank – against the backcloth of the snow-splashed Cairngorms. With the aid of Desmond Nethersole-Thompson, a fine field ornithologist and remarkable man, whose father had taught both my brothers at Latymer, we explored the higher moors for golden plover and dunlin, and the tops for dotterel. One evening our recording car ran aground in a lonely glen. On one side was a steep slope and on the other a fifty-foot drop down to a burn. We could not lift the vehicle or pack material under the wheels. It was nearly dusk and Bob and I were getting a little anxious. Then I looked down the track; there were two tiny figures plodding towards us. Then came two more – then a thin grey line! Sixteen people were walking up into the mountains at a time when most people would have been coming down. They were all men carrying packs which they soon discarded. They lifted the vehicle, turned it and pointed it towards base and put it down on the right side of the hole. All of them were making their way up to see the dawn rise on a chosen peak. It was the only evening when such help was possible – the evening before the longest day!

One morning early in July 1953 I climbed up into the hills with a frame on my back to which were strapped a portable tape recorder, a hundred yards of microphone cable, two mikes, a transformer, six reels of tape, an eighteen-inch reflector, maps and compass, food, drink and extra clothing. After a strenuous four-and-a-half-hour climb I stood in the world of the high tops. At a height of 3200 feet was a male dotterel on a single egg. I placed the reflector about twelve feet from the nest. The male was soon joined by a larger, more highly coloured hen who took a dominant part in the courtship and would leave her mate to incubate and rear the young. So tame were these very rare birds, known in earlier times as 'Mossfools', that I was able to sit out in the open only twenty yards from the nest scrape. All the time the birds were altering their positions with excited trillings and it was clear that the hen would soon lay the second egg. It was still and blisteringly hot on the exposed summit. A bee buzzed past the microphone. About half an hour after I had settled myself on a bed of golden moss the hen dotterel, whose bill had been open for some time as she panted in the heat, left the cock on the nest and walked over to the parabolic reflector. She examined it and then realizing that this round object provided the only shade on the bare mountain top, she moved in close and squatted down within three inches of it!

During our 1953 visit the call of the golden eagle had eluded us, but this disappointment merely strengthened our desire and resolve to come back to this magnificent land of mountain, loch and sky. So in May 1957 we returned for another summer. Colonel J. P. Grant of Rothiemurchus, who had befriended us four years earlier, now very generously put the Old Manse with its many facilities at our disposal. Here in the old Caledonian Forest we made the first recordings of the Scottish crossbill, grey wagtails, goosander flight calls and the songs of goldcrest and pied wagtail. By Loch Morlich, still secluded and unspoilt, we taped the stirring display of the male greenshank, the calls of teal and many lovely atmospheric sound pictures which I often play to myself to evoke the loneliness of those distant lochs and moors. I am especially fond of one recording I made by the little loch close to Drumintoul Lodge; in the background are the whispers of goldcrest songs and in the foreground the evocative 'plop' of trout rising on a still mountain evening. I also stayed with the late John Clark at Achlean and from his farmhouse in Glen Feshie I set out to climb Carn Ban Mor in a search for ptarmigan and their curious croaking cackle. One day I climbed up into a bitter sharp world of swirling mist and cold wind; the next day I was burned by the sun, despite four continuous weeks of outdoor work. Such are the Highlands, even in summer!

Bob and I took up our quarters in a remote bothy not far from a golden eagle's eyrie. This was situated over a thousand feet up a 1600-foot cliff face. It was necessary to man-haul 1800 feet of cable from the recording vehicle, which was to be our hide, up the mountainside. As I pulled the cable, in linked, roped sections, higher and higher, the weight increased and the climbing became more difficult. The eyrie itself was on a buttress and the last thirty feet with all that cable were to prove very severe. Only by prodding myself upwards with such remarks as 'It's your life ambition! Stick at it!' did I finally clamber up to the eyrie. Here, out of breath, I collapsed on the edge of a huge platform of sticks, much to the surprise of its only occupant – a young eaglet. I then had to go down and bring up the reflector. In a strong aroma of ripe game from several plucked and browning red grouse and mountain hares, I fixed the reflector with rope to stones which I jammed into a deep rock crevice. I then angled the reflector to point down at the eaglet and to stop rainwater running into the microphone. It would be a long climb back for a very small adjustment.

We were able to record the insistent hunger cheepings of the eaglet and, most exciting and rewarding of all, the tooting bark of the hen bird, which seemed out of keeping with its size and grandeur. The hen used to come over the mountain pass at a great height on a recce. If she thought that the area was clear, she closed her wings and plummeted down for 2000 feet before spreading her great pinions to float and peer down once more. If she was satisfied, the wings were folded once again and she dropped like a black boulder to rocket into the eyrie with a great rush of wings. It was quite breath-taking to watch and, of course, to record. The hen fed the eaglet with small strips of flesh while intimate and touching conversations took place between them.

In autumn the Cairngorms are beautiful with high snow and the golden birches set against the deep bottle-green of the Scots pines. In late September and October the rut – the mating – of the red deer takes place and from the basin of Rothiemurchus it is possible to hear the stags roaring high up on Castle Hill and in the Lairig Ghru pass. In one deer sanctuary we were able to make recordings of the deep-bellowed roarings and cracked bovine calls as red deer stags uttered their challenges and marshalled the hinds into more manageable groups. I crawled to within twenty feet of one fine stag and we recorded his loud roarings and a short gruff bark. In the sanctuary our guide was an old stalker of great experience, Finlay Macintosh. On a settee in his cottage was a fine tiger skin; I asked him how he had come by it. It seems that a certain Maharajah had arrived for a deer shoot with half a dozen secretaries. Conversations between him and Finlay had to be routed through all the secretaries, back and forth, on the open moor. No deer were shot.

'What's wrong?' demanded the potentate.

'Perhaps,' Finlay replied very gently, 'it might be possible for my suggestions and instructions to go through just one, or even two of your staff!'

'Let's try it,' ventured the Maharajah.

They stalked a fine stag and he got a good clean shot. 'You must come to India as my guest for six months,' enthused the Maharajah, and there, from the back of an elephant, Finlay got his tiger.

I have always been attracted by seabirds and these have led me to many beautiful and remote coastlines and islands. The Farne Islands off the coast of Northumberland were the goal of several expeditions for kittiwakes, shags, puffins, guillemots and terns. The Arctic terns on the Inner Farne drove their bills quite savagely into the back of my head, drawing blood, before rolling forward to avoid breaking their necks. I wanted to record the high-pitched screams and rattling machine-gun-like notes which accompanied the attacks, but, as they always came from behind, I was not able to swing the microphone fast enough to keep up with the diving terns. I asked a student who was staying on the Inner Farne if he would act as a target while I stood with the reflector a short distance away. This he said he would do 'in the cause of science' and we soon had some first-class recordings. Only when we had finished did I discover that he was not interested in birds and could not stand terns at any price!

The Farne Islands are an important breeding station of the Atlantic or grey seal and after years of protection their numbers have increased enormously. Today this has led to overcrowding, pup mortality and disease. In November 1955 Bob and I made a difficult landing from a coble on a sea-swept ledge on the Brownsman; the bow of the boat was rising and falling six or seven feet opposite the rocky platform. We lived in the old cottage where Grace Darling spent eleven of her girlhood years. We had brought our own water supply, coal, sleeping bags, food, recording gear and a petrol generator to recharge the batteries – thirty-three packages in all. Many migrant birds were coming over the North Sea – thrushes, starlings, finches, skylarks, woodcock, snipe and herons. As we stood in the doorway of the cottage, wedged between the eighteenth-century coal-fired watch tower and the round base of the later stone lighthouse, we could hear the strange haunting songs of the cow seals which had hauled up on Staple Island next door. Soon more seals were coming up the slopes of the Brownsman and we recorded a 600-pound bull, puffing and blowing his way into a seaweed-covered cove. Here he was joined by several spotted cow seals, one of which gave birth to a creamy-yellow pup covered with a soft silky fur. When it was two days old it would call to its mother with long anxious wails and the cow would answer from the sea with a mournful 'song' which sometimes dissolved into a bubbling gasp as she sank below a wave.

I watched a pup being born – a process that took no longer than fourteen seconds – but a wave swept it off a ledge into the sea where its coat soon became waterlogged. It took the cow about twenty minutes to breast the unfortunate baby forward into a crack where she suckled it for the first time. If we approached a young pup as he lay on his back, he would roll over and hiss loudly while huge tears welled up from his eyes and ran down his face. It was delightful living among these animals and my days on the Brownsman, cut off from the mainland by rough water where seals and killer whales swam, were some of the most satisfying in my life.

In our recording work we had always been hampered by the need to use cables and this was clearly demonstrated in some of the early techniques that we had used to record the peregrines and golden eagles. Bob and I therefore experimented with a light-weight pack-set transmitter and receiver with a built-in battery power supply. After a series of trials at Minsmere we were able in 1954, during a visit to Sir Peter Scott's Wildfowl Trust at Slimbridge, to record white-fronted geese at a range of a thousand yards from the recorder and without cables. In the following year we increased the range to one mile to record snow buntings on the seawall near Cley at Billy Bishop's house in the village. The results were of full broadcasting quality. I also spent several nights on the gallery of the old Dungeness Lighthouse in Kent with a microphone and transmitter. When I felt it in my bones that there was going to be a lighthouse night – that is one when migrants would appear around the lantern – I used to ring up Herbert Axell, then the warden of the Dungeness Observatory, and say, 'If it's all right, I'd like to come down for the nights of 6 and 7 October.'

His answer was usually forthright and meant, 'Don't be silly! I can't guarantee anything for those nights!' But Joan Axell always had a warm welcome and a bed, and, strange as it may seem, the nights I chose weeks before always turned out to be 'lighthouse nights'.

From the gallery of the light, with the faint roar of the paraffin lamp and outside a deep infinity of darkness broken by the searing yellow beams that slowly turned around my head, I could hear the calls of migrating golden plover or blackbirds and redwings, song thrushes and starlings, while robins, skylarks, lapwings, chiffchaffs and wheatears were often caught in the beams. One night in October 1957 we recorded by radio link the calls of goldcrests – needle-points of sound – as the birds came in from the sea and the darkness to pitch on the gallery rails and even on my head and shoulders. Herbert and

I boxed them up for later examination and one bird that I gently picked off my sleeve proved to be the much rarer firecrest.

Soon after I was appointed to the BBC it seemed that the London Zoo might provide some useful wildlife material for the Sound Archives, although recordings in the wild are often more valuable. I approached George Cansdale and permission was given for me to visit the zoo early in the morning when traffic noise was less and the public were not admitted. I secured recordings of many kinds of bird but I was anxious to concentrate on mammals, reptiles and fish which were poorly represented in the Archives. The cats were sullen and full of threat – the eastern Asiatic fishing cat, the sand cat from the Middle East, the handsome Indian leopard cat, Geoffroy's cat from South America which sounded just like a heavy piston-engined aircraft taking off and the ocelot which called quite clearly, 'No! No! No!' Then there was the lithe and graceful caracal lynx whose sharp warnings I obtained by entering his cage, holding him at bay with a large broom and pushing a microphone tied on a long pole under his nose. It took three years to get the sound of a jaguar, but 'Tubby' performed just in time for a play that Rayner Heppenstall was producing in which a vocal jaguar was a key figure. I was also able to keep for posterity the very strange singing and wailing noises that were produced when Rota, Sir Winston Churchill's famous lion, was mating in the early morning.

I also added the vocal sounds of the London Zoo's elephants and hippos, but I failed dismally with the sound of an elephant's heartbeat which was needed for a schools programme which Professor W. S. Bullough was presenting shortly. I climbed and crawled about, pushing and prodding a microphone into an Indian elephant's mammary fat, armpit and ribs. The zoo's veterinary officer, Oliver Graham Jones, came along to try to locate a pressure point, but also without success. My reward from a bored elephant was a faceful of sawdust surreptitiously acquired when I was looking the other way.

I became a great friend of Spike – the orang-outang – who died so sadly in the TB epidemic that hit the Monkey House. He used to hold my hand and take me on a personally conducted tour of the house. One recording showed the way in which the intonation and timbre of his keeper, William (Bill) Peckett, were reflected in the great ape's responses. Poor old Spike was a very dear animal. Guy, the gorilla, was only a youngster when I first met him and saw him wrestling with headkeeper L. Smith in his cage. I was able to record his laughing and chuckling as his palms were tickled – a practice that like many children he thoroughly enjoyed. One morning I was passing the widely spaced bars of his inside cage at corridor level when I saw his hand move back sharply before propelling a dark object through the bars and obviously at me. As I was accustomed to fielding at first slip on the cricket field, I plucked the missile from the air as it sailed past my ear. It was a small hard pear. Almost without thinking I threw it back at his broad black chest but without a great deal of force. He looked at me in surprise, retreated to the far corner of the cage and placed one hand over his eyes. Then he peered over the tops of his fingers, quite nonplussed. He never did it again.

The privilege of entering the London Zoo in the early mornings was a delightful one. I was often the first person to walk into the Monkey House, where I would be greeted with an ecstatic chorus of screams, chatters and banging on iron hatches. I watched operations on lionesses by Oliver Graham Jones and I held snakes which were warm and gentle and powerful young crocodiles in front of BBC microphones.

Fishes can produce sounds through their air bladders – these are hollow or drum-like – or by rubbing their gill teeth or pelvic girdle together to produce rasps, scrapings, scratchings and whines. In the summer of 1955, through the help of Deryck Chesterman, an old friend of my brother Thomas, and the Admiralty I was able to borrow a set of hydrophones. Bob was able to make up a suitable transformer to fit our high-performance tape recorder. The underwater response was very good and on one occasion, after we had left a hydrophone in one of the tanks of the London Aquarium after opening time, we clearly heard through three feet of air, a thick slab of armour-plate glass and four feet of water a feminine voice saying 'Coo! What's that thing hanging in the water?' After some carp and chubb had been deprived of food for a short time, I lowered a hydrophone into their tank while scraps of food were dropped on the water. The hungry fish broke the surface and produced extremely melodious whining or singing sounds lasting for half a minute or more. These seemed to be threat or warning calls and, as far as I know, were the first underwater fish recordings to be made in this country.

By preserving sounds on tape they are always available for study. My own pioneer recording work was carried out for a broadcasting organization and it was the potential programme use that I had to bear in mind. I did analyse many of the recordings in the only way open to me – by playing them at slow speeds. Halving the replay speed brought the pitch down an octave so that it was possible at one-eighth speed to listen to the pattern and shape of a bird song in a leisurely way. By slowing down the recording of the nightjar's vibrant churring I found that there were often as many as 1900 notes produced in a minute while the reeling trill of the grasshopper warbler could conceal 1400 double notes in one minute. As I was anxious that there should be a wider scientific use of the recordings it was decided that copies should also go to Cambridge and the British Trust for Ornithology. Many of my recordings of song and sub-song were later put through a sound spectrograph which, by using different filters, breaks down sounds into their constituent frequencies and provides a permanent visual record of pitch differences set against time. Pictures of a number of bird sub-songs that I had obtained were reproduced in a scientific paper by Dr W. H. Thorpe and P. M. Pilcher in *British Birds*.

The naturalist today devotes time to catching birds to examine, ring and release them, to studying them in the field, to photographing and filming them, and to making sound recordings of them. However, there are attendant dangers. I utterly deplore the way in which bird-watchers can harass tired, newly arrived migrants to get fleeting glimpses of them by constantly forcing them out of cover. In 1973 I came across an Englishman in the Camargue beating his way with a stick across a breeding colony of pratincoles and black-winged stilts after leaving a great reed warbler's nest completely open to view. I hope also that all those research workers who handle birds in the course of their professional studies will remember that they are not just statistics, but living things. In some ways the birds now need protection from the bird-watchers! For me the welfare of the birds has always come first. On many recording expeditions I have had to contend with the hazards of the weather, demanding climbs, deep mud, aircraft and traffic noise and the unpredictability of nature, but, as I wrote in *Voices of the Wild* in 1957, all these factors help to make wildlife sound recording 'the most glorious sport of all'.

11

Nature on the Air

My first broadcast after joining the BBC was in May 1951 and took place in a programme called *The London Countryside*, based on recordings made in Kensington Gardens and Hyde Park. I shared the presentation with C. Gordon Glover – the start of a professional relationship that was to last until his death in 1975. Born in Edinburgh, Gordon Glover had become broadcaster, novelist, writer of short stories and radio plays and a skilled and witty raconteur. He had a deep love of nature and the open spaces of the earth.

In 1951 I felt that despite the existence of the West Region programmes *The Naturalist* and *Birds in Britain*, devised by Desmond Hawkins, there was also room on the air for a programme that reflected life in the British countryside 'as it had actually happened'. I therefore worked out a plan for a series of monthly programmes based on recorded actuality in the countryside and illustrated with spoken contributions describing the events of the past month. Kenneth Adam, then Controller of the Light Programme and later Director of BBC Television, liked the idea and offered me twelve firm bookings at the end of each month of 1952. Gordon Glover was invited to write the linking material in what the *Listener* once called 'lush, poetic language'. I was to edit the programme and contribute items on natural history and Bernard Lyons was to produce it. I spent two whole weeks in the BBC's Gramophone Library searching for an appropriate signature tune – a distinctive piece of music suitable for sun, snow, wind, fog, long days, long nights, harvest and seed-time. I finally chose the incidental music called 'Music for the Rivers of the North of England', composed by Lambert Williamson and played by the BBC Northern Orchestra under Charles Groves. The music, which is not commercially available, has now been played on the air nearly 500 times.

I launched a preview of the new *Countryside* series in December 1951 in *Flashes of Light* which was introduced by Kenneth Adam and Franklin Engelmann, whom we all knew with affection as 'Jingle', and the first of more than 250 programmes was broadcast on 30 January 1952. David Lloyd James had a spell of two years or so narrating the programme and in 1954 Arthur Phillips became the regular producer until he retired after forty-five years' service with the BBC in 1974. I have been fortunate not to miss taking part in a single edition and have also narrated the whole programme on occasion. I have trekked from the Isles of Scilly to Fair Isle and from Upper Lough Erne to the Farne Islands to collect material. Ancient customs, fairs, farming, weather and many other aspects of our countryside were all featured as well. It has apparently become according to Paul Ferris of the *Observer*, 'a minor institution like Mr Middleton or Freddie Grisewood in their time'. After C. Gordon Glover's death early in 1975 Wynford Vaughan-Thomas was invited to write the linking narration and introduce the programme.

As I collected more wildlife recordings I was able to present programmes to introduce them and, in those days of more flexible planning, at quite short notice if the story was newsworthy. For the first time it was possible to relate the vocabulary of birds and other animals to their behaviour – badger language in *Science Survey*, the stone curlew and the peregrine on the Third Programme, and the little ringed plover with John Parrinder. After my 1953 expedition to record crossbills Alec Robertson and I sat in the Pavilion at Lord's to plan a joint radio script on those enigmatic birds as we watched the Australians. In those days there were also many other outlets for material, and I was invited to Bristol to take part in *The Naturalist* and *Birds in Britain*.

My association with *Woman's Hour* began in February 1952 when Jean Metcalfe interviewed me and the repeat was introduced by Robert Dougall whom I had met during my recording visits to Minsmere, many years before he became President of the RSPB. I began to broadcast regularly on children's programmes, including one series which was edited and produced by Lionel Gamlin – the former BBC anouncer, compère of *In Town Tonight* in the 1930s and chief commentator for British Movietone News. I also took part in *Children's Hour*, and Felicia Elwell, who was producing the Schools nature study series, asked me to undertake programmes for her on human and animal language.

Many of my lunchtimes in the 1950s were passed in the George in Mortimer Street where I regularly met Brian George and we were often joined by Ted Kavanagh, who wrote scripts for *ITMA* that sustained us during the war, Stanley Maxted of Arnhem fame and Wynford Vaughan-Thomas of the choice and telling phrase. One of my great friends was Robert Reid – in my opinion one of the very best of the war correspondents whose name will always be linked with his commentaries on the Battle of Normandy and on General de Gaulle's dramatic entry into Notre-Dame. Arthur Phillips often joined me for these convivial occasions.

Many producers of plays asked for advice and even new recordings so that their productions could be illustrated with authentic sounds and wildlife recordings, correct for place, time and season. It was no good playing a woodpigeon song for an African desert or South American rain forest! On one occasion actor Peter Coke, who was then playing Paul Temple, had written a radio thriller in which a Siamese cat played a vital role, but unfortunately there were no recordings of these animals. The actress Ann Codrington agreed with the producer, Ayton Whitaker, with whom I shared many lunchtime strolls bird-watching in Regent's Park, to offer her champion cat Mill Feather and her kittens for recording. Charles Lefeaux, who was producing C. S. Forester's *African Queen* with Celia Johnson and Deryck Guyler in the star roles, asked me if I would prepare a range of suitable jungle sounds to cover the eighty-five minutes of action.

The Corporation also agreed to my advising on the sound tracks of three films made by the British Transport Commission's Film Unit. The first was *Journey into Spring*, which was shot in Gilbert White's Selborne. Produced by Ian Ferguson and directed by Ralph Keene for Edgar Anstey, it also carried a commentary by Laurie Lee. It was a delightful film, in exquisite colour, reflecting the changes from the snow-bound woods and fields of March to the full glory of early summer. Shown first at the Odeon, Leicester Square, this Selborne film went on to win a full circuit release, the British Film Academy's award for the best documentary in 1957 and a nomination for a Hollywood Academy Award. The second film, *Between the Tides*, won first prize for an educational film at the Venice Film Festival in July 1958. The third film was *Wild Highlands* and I certainly learned a great deal about film-making from Edgar Anstey and the other members of his film unit. David Attenborough, who was about to embark on his great series of *Zoo Quest* films for television, came to talk about wildlife recording techniques with me and Ellery (Bill) Anderson, who led the Falkland Islands Dependencies Survey Expedition to the Antarctic in 1954, came to the London Zoo with me to practise recording before his departure south.

In the 1950s I also took part in a number of broadcasts on the BBC's Overseas Service. One series was called *This is Britain* and was introduced by Richard Dimbleby, who used to interview me in each programme about natural history in the British countryside, while I played new wildlife recordings. Richard was a genuine, amiable and very alive man, totally professional and always keeping faith with his listening audience by meticulously preparing his subject and background material. It was a real pleasure to work on a series with him. I always remembered his advice to me. 'Eric! When they start to walk on your face, then it's time to get out!' Later, when Dimbleby moved on to television and *Panorama*, his place in the series was taken by E. V. H. Emmett, who used to present Gaumont British News.

For part of my career on the staff in radio I had an office in Broadcasting House, but I later moved to an eyrie in Rothwell House in New Cavendish Street, now rehabilitated as flats. My new office was part of a small, intimate complex of rooms which I shared with Peter Kennedy and Seamus Ennis – those indefatigable collectors of folksongs – Harold Rogers, now manager of Radio Medway, and Humphrey Burton, who became head of the BBC's Music and Arts Department, then editor and presenter of London Weekend Television's much-acclaimed programme *Aquarius*, and in 1975 rejoined the BBC as head of Arts Features. Also housed in Rothwell was Laurence Gilliam's Features Department from which many notable programmes emerged over the years. From 1941 the poet Louis MacNeice, who had been a freshman at Merton in 1926 with my brother Thomas, had been a member of Features Department and it was during this period that he wrote *The Dark Tower*. Another Mertonian in the BBC at this time was the future Director-General, Hugh (later Sir Hugh) Carleton Greene, who was one year senior to my brother Wilfrid. I first met the D-G at a Mobile Recording Engineers' party in Hallam Mews – surely the best of the old Christmas parties in the BBC. A few years later he visited Penistone, where Wilfrid was headmaster, to give the prizes away – 'My first speech day!' he disclosed; he was the first Director-General to have risen from the staff. In 1975 I to was the Guest of Honour there.

During this time I was giving many lectures throughout the country and one which I particularly remember was in February 1953 to the British Ornithologists' Club. It was to be a study of the conversational and very subdued calls of birds made possible by the new techniques of recording I had introduced. Sir Philip Manson-Bahr, then the leading consultant in tropical medicine and a devoted ornithologist, took the chair. Colonel Meinertzhagen, who was sitting next to Thelma and propping up his hearing aid, not having ever heard me lecture before, leaned towards her and enquired in a kindly and paternal way, 'Will he be all right?'

I have already made it clear that I was working for a broadcasting organization and that it was not possible for me to take up many of the scientific issues that arose as I went along. For this reason I was very pleased to be invited to deliver a series of six University of London Extension Lectures at the newly formed British Institute of Recorded Sound where, under its hard-working secretary Patrick Saul, it was planned to keep a national collection of gramophone records available to research workers in the same way as books are stored in the great libraries. The lectures were about the language of birds

For the programme *Highland River* we carried film equipment deep into the Caledonian Forest, 1959. (*From left*: cameraman Eric Deeming, his assistant Peter Hall, and ES)

Thelma, David and Amanda. Stanmore Common, 1974

On location at Great Tew with Susan and Paul for the film series *A Year in the Country*, 1961

With film cameraman Charles Lagus *left* and his assistant Eddie Best near the summit of Sgoran Dubh Mor in the Cairngorm Mountains, 1963

Dr Roger Bannister demonstrating cardiac output in my programme *The Athlete's Triumph,* 1965

The late Maxwell Knight *right* introducing Rufus Creed and his tame vixen in a television programme I produced in 1961

Female black rhinoceros and calf in the Ngorongoro Crater

The Murchison Falls in Uganda, 1965

Scene on the River Nile near Paraa, 1965

Hippopotamus on a Nile mudbank, 1965

Top Outdoor sound location shooting at Rob Roy's cottage, Glen Shira, for the series *A Year's Journey*, 1970. (*From left*: cameraman Bill Munn, with assistant cameraman and sound recordist)

Above Indoor filming in the BBC News Studio in Broadcasting House, London, 1965. (*From left*: assistant sound recordist, sound recordist, Felicia Elwell (producer), producer's assistant, cameraman, assistant cameraman, ES, lighting engineer)

Top Filming *The Sands of Dee* with Norman Ellison — Nomad of the BBC *left*, assistant cameraman Ian Kennedy at 'big Bertha' and cameraman Sid Davies with exposure meter, 1966

Above With cameraman Phil Law on a Breton oysterboat returning from the island of Gavrinis, 1971

Top Interviewing Sir Peter Scott for the weekly World Service programme *Nature Notebook* in Bush House, 1968

Above Being interviewed by Derek Jones and recorded by producer Dilys Breese, with Sue Coates standing by, for *The Living World* programme on the wildlife of Neasden. The Welsh Harp, 1972 and other animals and Sir Julian Huxley, whom I regularly met on a BBC advisory committee, agreed to take the chair.

I was a member of the Royal Society for the Protection of Birds in the days when its headquarters were at 82 Victoria Street, and the society and its secretary, Philip Brown, had given me enormous help in visiting their reserves to make recordings. In 1953 I was elected to the Council of the RSPB – the same year that the society moved to its new premises in Ecclestone Square. The chairman of the Council at this time was Lord Hurcomb, former Director-General of the Ministry of Shipping from 1939 and, after the last war, chairman of the Transport Commission, and an outstanding naturalist and conservationist. Thelma and I recall with pleasure the delightful At Homes that he regularly gave in his Campden Hill apartments. I served on the general purposes committee and the film sub-committee, as I was particularly interested in the educational work of the society.

The years that I spent in radio from 1951 to 1957 saw the publication of two books of mine and a number of papers and articles. With the assistance of the BBC I was also responsible for two sets of bird recordings. The first was a series of six disks which I prepared, with commentaries, as a 'talking book' for the Royal National Institute for the Blind – a very rewarding and enjoyable task. The second set of recordings was *Witherby's Sound Guide to British Birds*, which provided recordings of nearly 200 species and was what Jeffery Boswall called 'the first effort towards a faunistic treatment'. It was devised by the late Myles North and myself and in the book accompanying the disks he describes how we maintained a long-distance correspondence of writings and tapes between London and Nairobi from 1953 onwards until the *Sound Guide* was ready in 1958, with its thirteen ten-inch 78 rpm records. I last saw Myles, one of the gentlest and kindest of men, in Kenya in 1966 and he did not live to see the LP version which was published in 1969.

12

Abroad for Birds

The Camargue! – a magical name for any ornithologist who knows that part of southern France which lies within the two arms of the great River Rhône before it flows fast and strong into the Mediterranean. It is a countryside of farms, small woods, shallow pools, reedbeds, arid wastes, beds of salicornia, ricefields and thickets of tamarisk where wild black bulls, white horses and wild boar roam at large and where many rare and beautiful birds breed. Inspired by George Yeates, Cézanne and Van Gogh, I persuaded the BBC to let me mount a recording expedition there in the summer of 1954. Bob Wade and I made our first port of call the house in Arles of M. Georges Tallon, who was the director of the *Société d'Acclimatation*'s three reserves. He granted us permission to stay at the old hunting lodge at Salin de Badon, deep in the wildest part of the Camargue. For a month we lived in the tall square house with its pink flush, set among fruit trees, pines, tamarisks and reeds.

During the early part of our stay we were assailed by the scourge of these parts – the mistral – that wind known as the Masterful One – which sweeps down from the colder north to lash the lagoons into white horses, to set the best of friends at each other's throats and to make all outdoor recording impossible. Then a morning dawned still and clear. In a region of low salicornia growth we recorded the song of a spectacled warbler whose territory had been marked out by M. Henri Lomont, the chief warden. A moustached warbler was singing near La Capelière in one of the reedbeds and a Cetti's warbler bombarded us with song from a nearby hedge. Then the mistral returned once more and blew without ceasing for almost a week. I used this trying, difficult time for finding new bird species and plotting territories and nests so that we could get to work as soon as the wind dropped. One morning the mistral was blowing its hardest and then in the afternoon it suddenly dropped. We started by recording a great reed warbler's song in a dyke near the house and the sparrow-like twitters of a melodious warbler in the garden. In the evening we managed to capture the low musical 'kius' of a pair of tiny Scops owls while thousands of frogs sang their great chorus from the stunted trees and waterways, and clouds of midges danced in the air. At La Capelière we taped the voice of the rare little crake and near Petit Badon we collected the first recordings of the penduline tit which hangs its beautiful bottle-shaped nest of reed fluff from the branches of the pink-flowered tamarisks. On the shores of the Étang de Vaccarès those aristocrats of the Camargue – the bee-eaters – were excavating their nesting holes. These are really fairy-like birds with long tail streamers, gold and chestnut backs, blue-green wings and tails and brilliant yellow throats. Another of the rare bird species that we had come all this way to find was the black-winged stilt – a black-and-white wading bird with absurdly long pink legs and a harsh yelping voice.

For a little while I had thought that there was a colony of purple herons in a reedbed on the other side of the Petit Badon road from the stilt colony. So I went and explored the marsh, clad in thigh boots and liberally spread with anti-mosquito cream. I gazed on reed-locked pools which may not have been seen by man for many years; here marsh harriers flapped and hovered in their search for prey and little bitterns clambered up the thin stems. The air was full of frog croaks, nightingales' songs and the notes of coot, moorhen, water rail, penduline tit and Cetti's warbler. I felt totally alone in the middle of the wilderness, with the reeds waving far above my head and the tamarisks spreading twisted jungles across my path. In the very centre of the marsh I found the nest-platforms of four pairs of breeding herons. Other herons were nesting in a great wood of parasol pines at the Mas de Sablons – little egrets, night herons and squacco herons – guarded by clouds of very aggressive and persistent mosquitoes. In the late 1960s that fine wood was deserted by the herons, perhaps because of growing disturbance, and a great ornithological spectacle was no more. And, of course, on the lagoons there were the flamingoes – *les flamants roses* – one of the strangest of Nature's inventions which I described in the opening chapter.

Staying with us at Salin de Badon was a young Spanish ornithologist, Don José Antonio Valverde Gomez, whom I came to know with affection as Tono. He was studying the little egrets and later wrote a distinguished paper on them. He also went to work at the Tour du Valat – the research station in the Camargue founded by Dr Luc Hoffmann. Here each week Bob and I were welcomed with a hot bath, a superb aperitif and an excellent dinner from our gentle, diffident host and his wife and this was a delightful change from the more spartan conditions at the hunting lodge. At Salin de Badon I also entertained the American ornithologist and artist Dr Roger Peterson and his wife Barbara. Roger was anxious, after filming penduline tits, bee-eaters and stilts in locations that I was able to suggest, to turn his attention to the flamingoes of the Camargue. Lord Alanbrooke had, in fact, given me a showing of his film of the flamingoes before I left England, but Roger was anxious to take his own material back to the United States. Under the guidance of Henri Lomont, Roger, Bob and I went to a second colony of these remarkable birds where some 430 pairs had their nests. At this time only one or two Englishmen before us had seen two flamingo colonies in Europe in the same year.

We explored the dry limestone hills of Les Alpilles, the hilltop village of Les Baux and the stony wilderness of La Crau. When we left the mysterious and beautiful land of Provence I had seen a total of 145 different species of bird and we had collected recordings of well over a score. Taking Tono Valverde with us we set off by road for Basel in Switzerland where I was to give a lecture to the XIth International Ornithological Congress on the conversational calls of birds – the first time that the BBC had been represented at such a gathering. My lecture was illustrated with recordings of stone curlews and crossbills, which Bob played off tape through a loudspeaker, and these intimate glimpses into the family language of birds were, like Heinz Sielmann's woodpecker film at the same congress, a new departure in ornithology. Even *Punch* took notice of the congress:

> Where Simms and Wade re-tune the crossbill's calls,
> And Kramer gives complacency a jolt
> With sun-steered mass migration; here there falls
> A stricken hush when Ingram speaks of moult.

For the first time the Russians were represented at a congress. As they had decided to come rather late, the proceedings had to begin much earlier each day to accommodate their talks, especially those by G. P. Dementiev and A. I. Ivanov. I was able to buttonhole **Dr** Ivanov, who spoke English, and ask him, 'Is any recording of birds going on in the Soviet Union?' His reply was 'No! Not yet!' and he was interested to hear of my own work. It was therefore a great pleasure some years later when Boris Veprintsev – the first Russian wildlife recordist to issue a commercial disk of bird sounds – sent me a personally autographed copy of his record. Thelma joined me for the congress and we lived for most of the time in a delightful hotel in sylvan surroundings at Bad Schauenburg among golden orioles, goshawks and middle spotted woodpeckers. Dr Ernst Lang conducted us round Basel Zoo – modern in outlook and design – and here Thelma and I had an entertaining tea with Professor J. B. S. Haldane and his wife Dr Helen Spurway; he was very interested in the new recording techniques and quizzed me hard about them.

'So largely abandoned to nature; nature in wildest primeval garb, untouched by man, untamed and glorious in pristine savagery.' These extravagant phrases from the pen of that great naturalist–hunter Abel Chapman described Spain and it was this richness in wildlife which brought Bob Wade and myself to that country in the summer of 1956.

We made our first base in Philip II's and Cervantes' home city of Valladolid. Our local guide was Tono Valverde's brother, Carlos, who was a taxidermist. Over glasses of cognac and my copy of *The Field Guide to the Birds of Britain and Europe* and with a liberal use of scientific names, French and Latin words strung together with gestures we planned our recording expeditions in Spain. We visited a strip of woodland along the banks of the muddy River Pisuerga not far from Valladolid which was full of migrant warblers, hoopoes, serins, Spanish green woodpeckers, nightingales and Cetti's warblers. A reporter from the local paper, the *Diario Regional*, got to hear of our strange exploits and came to ask if he could join us on a recording trip.

'Of course!' I assured him, 'but it will mean an early start!'

'What, about half past nine in the morning?' he enquired.

'No! Half past five,' I replied.

'But that's the middle of the night!' he complained. But he was there early the next morning and listened to a playback of our recordings.

In the open pinewoods of Castile we recorded great spotted cuckoos – magnificent birds with shrill rasping calls, and there were rock sparrows around the farm buildings, short-toed larks over the great savannah at Overuela and black kites at Cabazon by the river. A sheer limestone cliff beyond the stream was the home of Egyptian vultures, peregrines and short-toed and booted eagles. At this time I was rather plagued with a sore throat and decided to visit a doctor friend of Carlos who invited me into his surgery complete with operating table, dentist's chair and rows of glass cabinets from floor level to ceiling, full of knives, scalpels, pliers and extractors. After a brief examination he only prescribed twenty-four throat pastilles and two suppositories. After that experience Bob and I came to an agreement that if one of us appeared to be at death's door the other would drive him to Madrid and put him straight on board the first BEA Viscount for London!

The time finally came for us to leave the dusty, superheated plain of Castile for the cool freshness of the Sierra de la Demanda and a remote Benedictine monastery. This was the Abbey of Santo Domingo de Silos, named after an eleventh-century monk, Dominic; it was used as a halt on the pilgrim route to Santiago de Compostela and became one of Christendom's most famous religious houses. The road to it was long and tortuous, winding its way beneath crags and rock pinnacles until it reached 6000 feet above sea level. Here the track flattened out and ran alongside a clear mountain stream. We arrived at the abbey in the low golden light of evening as its great wall and towers cast long shadows over the village crouching at its foot. At the lodge we received a warm welcome and were then taken to comfortable apartments and shown some of the finest flush lavatories in Spain. The monks insisted on waiting on us and we were cared for exactly as St Benedict had instructed: 'Let all guests who come to the monastery be entertained like Christ himself, because He will say "I was a stranger and ye took me in".'

The countryside around Silos was full of running streams and lush water meadows blossoming with cowslips, kingcups and grape hyacinths. This paradise was graced by many wagtails of the Spanish race, woodchat shrikes, woodlarks, whitethroats and melodious warblers. Groves of poplar thrust up their green crowns and from them came a chorus of singing serins, redstarts and golden orioles. Pines grew up the mountain slopes and gave shelter to red-legged partridges, rollers, green woodpeckers, crested tits, cuckoos, and rock and ortolan buntings. Set in this wild countryside was the abbey. Here we approached the refectory along the lower of two tiers of cloisters which had been built by St Dominic about the year 1070. The columns on the ground-level arcades bore capitals ornamented in the most varied and delicate way. There were horned harpies and dogs fighting off eagles, combats between lions and eagles, and birds in courtship display. There were also many biblical scenes.

I often used to stand and admire the pillars and also the two great cypress trees where goldfinches were singing and the fountain in the courtyard from which silver drops cascaded over green cushions of moss where midwife toads were lying concealed and ringing their fairy bells.

The abbot – a tall, ascetic man – washed our hands before we sat down to meals of soup, meat or fish, bread and cheese, served with a bottle of red wine. The monks observed the rule of silence during the meal, but one of them read to us from a pulpit in the wall. Father Saturio, the eighty-four-year-old founder of the Silos Museum, was an outstanding ornithologist, taxidermist and archaeologist, as well as the creator of a secret and superb liqueur which he only made he said 'for the sake of the monks' health'! Much younger was Father Laurentino, who ringed the young storks on the bell tower each year, accompanied us on several field trips and supplied marvellously varied picnics and bottles of wine for each outing. He once took me on a truly hair-raising climb up a cliff in the Yecla gorges in search of eagle owls.

At these higher levels the bare rock slopes and faces were also the home of black redstarts, rock thrushes and black wheatears; once I had a superb view of a male wallcreeper – a study in crimson and black and a very rare bird in this part of Spain. The crags were occupied by nesting lesser kestrels, ravens, choughs, jackdaws, rock doves, alpine swifts, crag martins and Egyptian and griffon vultures. In one hot, dusty valley some miles away I watched thirty griffons and three Egyptians in the air at once. Bob and I climbed one rock face in a blazing sun and, as we did so, hordes of griffons began to pour out from their nest holes. I counted no fewer than eighty-seven soaring on broad pinions over my head – one of the great moments of my life. We found a high ledge and settled ourselves behind some tiny stunted trees which gave us some concealment from the vultures; here we set up our recording gear. As the griffons began to come back they passed low over our heads with a loud whooshing noise and soon the whole cliff face was reflecting the sound of rushing wings. We had to wait for another four hours before one of the birds uttered a few guttural croaks, but these few seconds of sound were sufficient reward for the relentless broiling that we underwent that day.

We played a number of our bird recordings to the monks, who were so excited that they invited me to make recordings of their plainsong – perhaps the finest in Spain. I would have liked to record the chants but was diffident about asking the monks direct. Now they offered them to us and I was delighted. So in the music practice room, with its piano and huge relief map showing all the Benedictine monasteries in the world, we were privileged to record the magnificent plainsong which few people outside Silos had heard, including the special 'Lamentacion de Silos'.

So far I had only seen the birds of northern Spain and I was anxious to visit Andalucia where the sun scorches the olive trees and orange groves. The road south took us along the valley of the Guadalquivir through huge olive groves and cornfields and over low hills where chocolate-coated cork oaks, white cistus and golden gorse grew in wild profusion. We began to see hedges of aloe and prickly pear growing around tiny cottages and it was in a cactus hedge near Montero that I saw my first rufous bush-chat. The road verges were a picture to delight the eye with pink mallow and lavatera, mauve iris, white asphodel, golden mustard, blue convolvulus and borage, made even more colourful by the bee-eaters hawking for insects above them. Two white storks were sitting on the great column to the Archangel Raphael in Cordoba and at the Moorish fortress of Carmona there were five griffons and a black vulture circling in front of a cliff. Sevilla was bright with camellias and roses and as we turned west we began to see cottages ringed with blossoming bougainvillaea under the shadow of tall eucalyptus trees with pale bark and silvery leaves set against a sky of the intensest blue. Montagu's harriers were beating above the fields and snow-white cattle egrets stalked among the cattle.

We finally settled in the Atlantic port of Huelva, made famous by the film *The Man Who Never Was*, and later we met the man who took 'Major Martin's' documents to Madrid. I had arranged to meet Peter Weickert, who lived in Huelva and knew a great deal about the wildlife of the province. The town itself was an important port for the shipment of ore and provided an interesting contrast of dusty dirt roads and new apartment blocks. It lay to the west of the Coto Doñana – a great wilderness of flood plain, sandy beaches, heath and wood. This area is rich not only in birds but in some of Europe's remarkable mammals – lynx, genet, mongoose and polecat as well as foxes, wild boar and fallow deer. It was to this sanctuary that Abel Chapman came nearly a century ago. It was to this same arid region that Guy Mountfort led his second expedition also in 1956 with Lord Alanbrooke, Eric Hosking, James Fisher, Roger Peterson and other ornithologists and which he described in his book *Portrait of a Wilderness*: in it he was kind enough to include a number of my observations from the western side of the Coto. Bob and I drove through Palos de la Frontera where Columbus is thought to have drawn his water and into a region of pine and heather on the edge of the Coto Doñana; this was a land of charcoal burners and large bluey-green ocellated lizards. I saw lots of azure-winged magpies and great spotted cuckoos, black kites, Sardinian and subalpine warblers and woodchat shrikes. We made our way over the dune country and through belts of stone pine, cork oak, tree heath and bracken to a long-stagnant lagoon – the Laguna de las Madres. I could hear reed, great reed and Savi's warblers singing in the reedbeds while grey and purple herons were feeding in the evil-smelling water; there were, in fact, ten pairs of breeding grey herons there and a smaller number of purple.

After tramping through the reeds I came to a clump of small trees and there I saw one of the great glories of the bird world – a breeding colony of little egrets, cattle egrets and night herons, some ninety pairs in all. Great clusters of stick-built nests filled the trees and bushes, while the branches were full of displaying, arguing, sleeping birds. A number of the nests had been robbed but there were young birds present who were being attended by a stream of arriving adults. Beyond the colony there were ten pairs of spoonbills nesting in the shorter reed growth and on the shallow pools, carpeted with water lilies and white ranunculus, were coot, mallard, and ferruginous duck.

This was also a land of iced soup and paellas, wines of fullness and asperity, and music and dance. We explored the Franciscan convent which sheltered Columbus and Cortez on his return from Mexico and we brought back a whole range of recordings of Huelva's fandangoes and flamencoes. On our long journey back to France across the sierras we could look back on a remarkable trip. We passed through the haunts of the lammergeier – the bearded vulture. Of all the European birds whose pictures I had pored over as a small boy, the lammergeier had taken pride of place. Now I was rewarded by the sight of one flying, fluent and masterful, along a towering cliff which thrust upwards towards a ceiling of grey cloud. On the wall of my study is a Christmas card from Colonel Meinertzhagen which is a reproduction of the magnificent embroidered portrait that he created of a lammergeier, sitting hunched and brooding on a lonely rock. The sight of the bird in the air was the crowning moment of my visit to Spain. Back in London I was interviewed by the Press about the expedition. One cub reporter listened with great interest as I gave an account of how we collected some fine recordings of Gregorian chants. Checking his story, he enquired, 'Do these ever fly to England?'

13

Television

The recording of wildlife in the field was without question the most fulfilling and enjoyable task that I have undertaken; it ideally suited my temperament and deep interest in animal communication, and it was one that I would have liked to continue to follow in the way which I had devised by 1957. We had a strong team, the latest electronic aids that the resources of the Corporation could provide, a specially designed vehicle and a folding boat with outboard motor. The BBC had even granted me a special award in March 1957 but shortly after this a decision was made to set up a natural history unit in Bristol to serve the needs of both radio and television – including the new schools television service – but it was 'not to be a monopoly'. After I came back from a lengthy recording expedition to the Scottish Highlands in the summer of 1957 I found that there was a proposal to transfer me to Bristol where, although some recording but little broadcasting work would be open to me, it was envisaged that I would become 'the presiding genius of the natural history and film library'. I had not originally joined the BBC for this type of work and still needed room for a creative output.

About this same time Felicia Elwell, who had transferred from the school radio service to the fledgling BBC schools television department, invited Bob Wade and myself to present a television film which would show how we set about recording bird songs and exploiting the material afterwards. I discovered that there was to be a vacancy for a production assistant in the new television department, and having failed to gain appointment to the senior producer post in Bristol I decided to apply for this post.

Television

My first assignment was to assist Felicia with her immediate series in the spring term of 1958 and with another series of ten programmes scheduled for the summer term. At this time the head of the department was Enid Love, who left early in 1959 for ITV; she was succeeded by Kenneth Fawdry, who was the senior education officer of the School Broadcasting Council which advised the Corporation on the schools department's output. The small staff in this new television venture in education included Donald Grattan, a future Controller, and Ronald Eyre, the distinguished writer and director of plays. Among later members were Michael Gill and Peter Montagnon, who produced the much-acclaimed *Civilisation* programmes with Sir Kenneth (later Lord) Clark.

I was soon sitting in a darkened television studio control room, directing cameramen and guiding Professor W. S. Bullough of Birbeck College through a series of programmes on *Animals with Backbones* which Felicia was producing. The summer term of 1958 was an important time for the new service and our secondary school series on birds was a high-powered and ambitious scheme. Felicia had invited the ornithologist and broadcaster James Fisher to present more than half of the series of ten programmes on birds; the others were to be introduced by Dr E. W. Swinton of the British Museum, John Barlee and myself, while two of the programmes – on bird-watching by Dick Bagnall-Oakeley and on birds' nests by Dr Bruce Campbell – were to be my sole responsibility. Four of the others I had to direct live on the air.

A programme might start as a few notes or headings on the back of an envelope during a train journey which could be reassembled rather more logically at a later date. Then a choice of presenter had to be made, usually by a process of elimination. Decisions then had to be taken as to whether the headings could best be illustrated by studio demonstrations and models, animated diagrams, existing or specially shot films, still photographs or drawings. The introduction could be a riveting film sequence, while dramatic shots might be used to give a breathing space in the programme after a rather didactic bit of presentation. Each piece had to be assessed for time and in this way a production would be built up. There would be many discussions with the speaker. Film sequences had to be directed or borrowed from existing sources and edited, models and special effects had to be commissioned, the set designed, captions ordered, illustrations blown up for display, still pictures photographed. Many planning meetings would take place involving the designer, the technical operations manager who was responsible for the cameras and technical facilities, the lighting and sound supervisors, the floor manager and the producer. I evolved a script with my speaker and in a quiet corner of the Television Centre or at home I worked on a camera script which contained all the camera moves, studio activities and projection of film involved in the production. During the first three and a half years of my ten-year association with schools television my studio programmes were always live – which troubled my nights and during transmission sped the adrenalin around my body in a rather alarming way.

In the autumn of 1958 the BBC decided to increase the number of its live television transmissions to schools from four a week to five and with two repeats. I went on a six weeks' television producer course with thirteen others including Stewart Morris, Terence Dudley and Keith Clement, who in 1974 put the spring General Election on the air, employing twenty-five monitors, eight cameras and twenty-four outside broadcast units. We all had to prepare our own production exercises on a minimal budget. I was paired with Donald McWhinnie, the assistant head of sound drama, who had had a great deal to do with the 'radiophonic workshop' and had specialized in the production of plays by Harold Pinter, Giles Cooper and Samuel Beckett. I acted as floor manager – the producer's interpreter and representative on the studio floor – for his exercise playlet and he reciprocated for my production. This I called *A Bird's Eye View* and it was a playful take-off of bird-watchers. I realized that this was probably my only chance to take a harmless and not unkindly dig at the bird-watching fraternity. Dick Bagnall-Oakeley agreed to present the programme and supplied me with film, including some new material that he shot for me of bird-watchers on the East Bank at Cley. Stanley Unwin came along to give aids to the recognition of bird-watchers' by the optical equipment that they carried. This first Field Guide to Bird-watchers with two such extrovert and amusing performers reduced the staff production secretary to hysterics so that in the end I had to grab the stopwatch from her hand in order to check the running time myself.

During the producers' course my father died at Badby after several months of the only real ill-health that he suffered in his long life. He was eighty-six. His last journey on earth was through the sunlit, honey-coloured villages of Northamptonshire where he had spent the last – and I think – happy years of his life. My mother, who cherished her independence, chose to stay on at the cottage in Badby where she had friends and where her family could reach her fairly easily.

My television life was divided between the world of the studios with their live programmes and expeditions to shoot new films or sequences. Early in 1959 I produced five twenty-minute studio shows called *Mammals in Britain* which were presented by John Sankey, Ernest Neal, Maxwell Knight, Professor Humphrey Hewer and Dr L. Harrison Matthews. I was able to call upon Ernest Neal's own film of badgers at night, of Professor Hewer's film studies of grey seals and a remarkable film that I obtained from Poland showing blindfolded bats flying through the meshes of a net, but, after being fitted with earplugs to upset their sonar, crashing right into it. Tom Driberg observed that 'Animals notoriously make the best television and the BBC's series *Mammals in Britain* has included some beautiful documentary material on seals, badgers and other beasts.' My first film editor was Barry Toovey, who became the supervising editor for the BBC's film epic on *The Great War*; his assistant was Jack Gold, whom I well remember making a short film at his own expense about an old folks' day trip to the seaside. This was the beginning of a great film career in which Jack directed such films as *The Bofors Gun*, *The Reckoning*, and what I consider to be one of the funniest films I have ever seen – *The National Health*.

Television production is essentially the result of good teamwork. Our resources also included animations and special effects, and the designers created atmosphere by their pleasing sets. One of my designers was Julia Trevelyan Oman, whose creations were seen in Jonathan Miller's production of *Alice*,

Alan Bennett's first play *Forty Years On* and the film *The Charge of the Light Brigade*. I also called on the services at various times of Robert Dougall, Judith Chalmers, and Meryl O'Keefe for announcements and trailers for the programmes.

In the summer of 1959 I produced a series on *The Insect World* which included a programme on ants by David Attenborough, and another on honey bees by Dr Colin Butler. The School Broadcasting Council and its sub-committees sponsored the BBC's output for schools, advising the Corporation on what the schools needed. The members included many teachers and representatives of educational authorities and organizations. We producers were also educationalists by background, explaining our proposals to the sub-committees, meeting with professionals working in the schools and visiting schools to see our own programmes go out on the air, if they were prerecorded. This lead to the kind of confusion which induced one small boy to enquire of me, 'How can you be here in the school and on the telly at the same time?' The education officers of the SBC viewed many of the programmes and their reports supplemented those from the reporting schools themselves. Our productions were also supported by sets of pupils' pamphlets and teachers' notes, the preparation of which was very time-consuming, but they were essential to the long-term value of what we were trying to do.

From the follow-up point of view our programmes were just as good as the teachers who took the viewing classes, but we were always trying to raise our standards. It has been argued that educational broadcasting is so specialized a resource that it should perhaps not be in the care of the BBC. Sir Charles Curran, the BBC's Director-General, gave a firm answer in July 1974 when he said: 'We have unique sources of information; immense technical facilities and skills; specialized production talents; access to performers, contributors, advisers and consultants; an inbuilt capacity for immediate response to, and reflection of events.'

I particularly enjoyed a series of bird programmes that I produced with the late Dick Bagnall-Oakeley – a fine and enthusiastic television performer who supplied his own superb films and could cope with electronic failures on the air with perfect equanimity. Dick was a highly professional performer and a good friend, and I remember the hilarious evenings that he spent with Thelma and myself before the programme days in Lime Grove or the Television Centre. I was responsible for natural history programmes in a very wide sense, so that I invited Dr Bruce Campbell to present a series on British trees and their timber use and wildlife, Percy Thrower a programme on plants, Maxwell Knight on animal signs and tracks, Professor W. S. Bullough on fossils and Dr John Carthy on the seashore. I explored the natural history of built-up areas with Dr Ernest Neal and two of the programmes were about my own garden in Dollis Hill in north-west London. These included some fine film of insects and garden birds specially shot for me by cameraman Geoffrey Mulligan.

We introduced quite a number of live animals to the studios. Fish, reptiles and amphibians came and went without great problems, but there were occasional difficulties. I remember the duck that sank like a stone in its tank, having somehow lost all its waterproofing – it had to be rescued in a hurry! And then there was the Chinese goose that made such a prolonged and hideous racket that it had to be removed from the studio, and the penguin which tried to run round the back of the television cameras. Chimpanzees seemed always to behave, but in a programme I produced about bats a large, smelly fruit bat fell off its pole on to the floor but no damage was done. I made it a general rule that I would film in advance any animal that might become fractious or appear frightened in the studio situation and thus cause anxiety or concern among the viewers.

In September 1961 I joined the 'adventure cruise' of the *Dunera*, now alas no more, and voyaged round the north-west mainland of Britain to the remote Scottish Isles. On charter to the National Trust for Scotland this 12 000-ton former troopship belonged to the British India Company and was used for educational cruises. We visited the Summer Isles, St Kilda, the Flannans, North Rona, Sula Sgeir, Lerwick, Fair Isle, the Isle of May – all names of wonder and magic for me! On board was a group of experts including two old friends of mine – Major the Hon. Henry Douglas-Home and film maker Christopher Mylne.

It was an exciting cruise in which we gazed on the ruins of the village on Hirta and the mighty cloud-topped precipice of Conachair. The *Dunera* even steamed through the 500-yard gap between Stac Lee and Boreray as a great cloud of gannets rose up into the sky. I counted the grey seals hauled up on North Rona and I feasted my eyes on bare, gaunt Sula Sgeir. The mailboat *Good Shepherd* came out from Fair Isle to greet us. On board the *Dunera* there were stimulating evenings with Gaelic authority Dr James Ross, who introduced me to a whole range of special whiskies, Alex Warwick, the Master of Works for the Trust, and Tam Dalyell, Member of Parliament since 1962 for West Lothian and deputy director of studies on board the *Dunera*. He was a great advocate of educational cruises and he described our Scottish cruise in his book *Ship School*. In recent years my son David has travelled with the *Nevasa* of British India to the Holy Land, Greece, Crete, Turkey and Egypt and my daughter Amanda went with the Guides on the same ship to Gibraltar, Lisbon and the Canary Islands. At the end of 1974 the *Nevasa* was withdrawn from service because of rising operating costs.

I had one more studio series to present. It was a contribution to the education of Sixth Forms. The overall title was *Science and Society* and the unit for which I was responsible – *Frontiers for Man* – was designed to show how man, and some other animals, could adjust to changing environments, including those of the sea and outer space. I was able to persuade a formidable team of experts to take part. Dr Otto Edholm, the head of the Division of Human Physiology at the National Institute for Medical Research in London, provided the background to human physiology and an account of his special researches into living in extremes of heat and cold. In the third programme Dr Roger Bannister – now Sir Roger – who ran the first four-minute mile and was a consultant neurologist to several London hospitals, talked about the psychological make-up of world-class athletes and the limits that the body may put on physical performance. Dr David Kerslake of the RAF Institute of Aviation Medicine at Farnborough presented *Man in Space* and in the final programme *The Challenge of the Sea* Surgeon-Rear Admiral Stanley Miles, the director of

Naval Medical Research, explored the strange world below the waves. I directed film sequences in the Farnborough decompression chamber and the Royal Navy loaned me some film, not seen on television before, of divers operating at great depth and breathing a mixture largely of helium.

Not all my television work was confined to the production side of the cameras. I took part in a number of live studio programmes and these included regular items to *Town and Around* – the local television news programme in London and the South-East. One item showed birds in my suburban garden and, another, very hungry redwings and fieldfares feeding on cotoneaster berries close to the Central Line trains running into the White City Station not far from my office in the Television Centre. On another occasion I reviewed Richard Fitter's *Collins Guide to Bird Watching*. Fortunately I was able to spend a few minutes briefing Richard before transmission, particularly as a girl appeared from nowhere and said 'Come this way!' only three minutes before the national news was due to end and our item, introduced by Michael Aspel, was due to start. We were ushered straight into the main news studio where Robert Dougall was reading the news. I steered Richard over the cables and round the back of the cameras, as Dougall gave me a glance of recognition, and into one of two chairs. The news ended and in no time I was on, introducing some new film of birds I had obtained in Oxfordshire, showing the book and talking to Richard Fitter. It was particularly disconcerting as automatic cameras rose, peered, craned and moved about by remote control. As soon as we were off the air a note was handed to me from Robert Dougall: 'Eric! Don't let Richard Fitter go yet! I want to meet him!'

14
Film-Making

For me, inspired early by John Grierson's *Drifters* and Robert Flaherty's *Man of Aran*, the making of films was preferable to studio television programmes. One had almost total control of the medium and thus the way in which one translated a series of ideas into interlocking moving pictures.

Between 1958 and 1967 I presented more than eighty films on the screen. In 1958 Felicia Elwell and I filmed all five of the Field Study Centres from Skomer to Malham Tarn. The location sequences were all linked together by me on one of the BBC television film studio stages at Ealing. I worked many times in what has been called 'London's little Hollywood', where for me there was still a touch of mystery and glamour about these stages on which I now performed and where such classics as *The Four Just Men, Kind Hearts and Coronets* and *Passport to Pimlico* were made. In 1959 Felicia and I jointly produced and I presented eight films showing the effect that water has had on our coasts and scenery and the interesting plants and animals that can be found in and around the sea and freshwater. Our first film was about the water cycle and was set in the caves in Cheddar Gorge, and Wookey Hole, and at the Chew Valley Reservoir. We had to film in the caves at night so as not to interfere with the daytime paying public and we also needed a large mobile generator to supply enough current to illuminate such wonders as Solomon's Temple, the grottoes curtained with pink stalactites, the eerie Witch of Wookey and the subterranean River Axe. At Wookey there are three great chambers through which the river flows; the innermost, where the stream disappears from view, has a span of 135 feet and a maximum height of only twelve. It was here, when the filming was over, the cables cleared away and the caves evacuated, that I sat alone in darkness to record on my tape machine the resonant and metallic tinkle of drops of water falling from the cave roof.

We followed the course of the River Allt Mor from Cairn Gorm to the River Spey and in contrast we made a film too about the Wiltshire Avon as it meandered through fertile water meadows to its estuary near Christchurch. I lined up through the viewfinder a beautiful shot of the Avon with poplars to the right, willows to the left and a mirror-like pool in the centre. Then the sun went in and the highlights of the scene disappeared. We waited twenty-five minutes for the sun to shine once more. 'Run!' I called to cameraman Eric Deeming and the camera began to turn.

After about seven seconds Eric shouted, 'What's happened to the shot? Shall I cut?'

'No! Keep running!' was my instruction, 'I'll tell you about it afterwards!' And what had happened was that an eight-pound salmon running upriver had jumped four feet out of the Avon right in the middle of the shot, splashed down and then risen again. Eric, looking through his ground-glass screen, thought that someone had thrown a brick in and spoiled his reflections. But what a sequence it turned out to be!

Other delightful locations included the Devon coast where we filmed shellfish, crabs, prawns and anemones in rock pools. But these were vertical shots looking downwards and so we arranged plastic tanks with weed and stones so that we could take horizontal shots of our subjects – bearded rocklings, butterfish, blennies and eels that I caught in the pools. For the first time we also filmed through a microscope so that we could show plankton – the larval forms of various marine animals – on the screen. At Blakeney Point which we visited with the warden Ted Eales we filmed terns and waders and the fascinating story of dune growth, and we went to the Farne Islands.

In 1961 came the biggest challenge that Felicia and I had yet faced – a new series of twenty-eight films of twenty minutes each, 'designed to encourage young children to explore their environment and find out for themselves how many fascinating things there are to discover even in quite ordinary places'. It was decided to set the films against the background of a definite village and the series was to be called *A Year in the Country*. We settled on the village of Great Tew in Oxfordshire, a few miles from Chipping Norton. With its thatched cottages, honey-coloured walls, medieval church, village smithy, school, stocks on the green and nearby farmland it was a delightful piece of rural England. The young and cultivated Lord Falkland, who died fighting for Charles I at the First Battle of Newbury, had lived here and the garden of the manor had been replanted in the nineteenth century by John Loudon, the landscape gardener.

The squire of Great Tew was Major Eustace Robb, a pioneer of television, who had just fought a wrathful battle against proposals to begin open-cast iron-ore mining in the area. Not far away was a mixed farm of just under 400 acres whose attractions, which we filmed, included the remains of a Roman villa, a Friesian milking herd, streams, ponds, hedges, copses and birds. The River Evenlode provided many valuable glimpses of all kinds of wildlife. With the help of two local children of primary school age, Susan and Paul, we reflected the daily life of the village, farm, countryside and river throughout a whole year. The two children were marvellous to work with and underwent the various disciplines of film-making with enthusiasm and equanimity despite inclement weather and long waits between shots. They made model farms, looked for fossils, collected autumn fruits, traced the course of rivers, searched under stones for small animals, took cycle tests with the local police sergeant, worked on the farm, built bird tables, weather vanes and arches, hunted the pond for aquatic insects and set up cages for caterpillars – nothing was beyond the ability of these two youngsters. One of our films, *The Coming of Spring*, was entered for the Japan Prize.

The series had been a long and demanding one, but, as I was based in Chipping Norton, I used to get up at half past five each morning to drive round the Cotswolds. In this way, over a period of twelve months, I visited every town, village and hamlet before the day's filming began. I was left with a lasting kaleidoscopic set of memories – of towns laid out below me in a wreath of morning mist, of swifts circling around the roofs of Lower Slaughter, of a late barn owl flitting along a hedgerow by the Saxon church of Coln Rogers, of water voles chewing quietly away in front of Arlington Row and of swallows flying in and out of the open door of Hailes Church. I climbed up to see the ancient long barrows of Belas Knap and Notgrove – 4000 years old and bright with rock roses, wild thyme and musk thistles and alive with singing larks, butterflies and drowsy humblebees. There was the magic of Cornwell's symmetry and the eeriness of the Rollright Stones. It had all been a great adventure. The whole series was re-broadcast between 1964 and 1965. Among the many remarks by children about the programmes I particularly like one from a girl which said, 'I thank you for the programme or we might have been doing arithmetic!'

In the summer of 1963 I directed a series of eight films which took viewers out into the British countryside and back through time to show how the natural scene had altered over the years. My subjects included the New Forest, Fenland, the Saxon open fields at Laxton, the Suffolk farm of Braggons, where I had worked as an undergraduate with Monica and Ken Laflin, and the birds of London which were featured in a film called *Concrete Desert*. For the first of the series I travelled with cameraman Charles Lagus and his assistant Eddie Best to the Fair Isle. Charles had many successful *Zoo Quest* films with David Attenborough under his belt and I found him a most professional, sympathetic and likable colleague. We reached the island, which lies between Orkney and Shetland, by way of Aberdeen, the MV *St Clair*, and a bus from Lerwick to Grutness Pier near Sumburgh. The Fair Isle mailboat *The Good Shepherd* carried us and our equipment through the dreaded waters of the Sumburgh 'roost' which have struck fear into the hearts of many travellers. My purpose in visiting the island was to make a film showing how the life of the forty or so islanders, by the nature of their existence, differed from that of people on the mainland. Fair Isle was remote and, at first, rather forbidding, with magnificent sea cliffs and stacks; here kittiwakes, auks, fulmars and shags nested in fantastic numbers while grey seals hauled up on the reefs below the precipices. We even rescued a lamb from a little beach, quite uninjured, that had survived a fall of several hundred feet. Fair Isle wrens, pale and rufescent, sang by the Observatory and on the slopes above the sea. Over the heather moor narrow-winged Arctic skuas, or 'skutialans', and huge buccaneering great skuas, or 'bonxies', came wheeling overhead, some to swoop savagely at us with our cameras and recording gear or to sweep in low about eighteen inches above the ground as they pressed home an attack before climbing steeply upwards above our heads.

We were blessed with days of sunny weather. The people of the island were warm-hearted and good-humoured, like many whose lives are hard and shaped by the elements. The men lived by crofting, fishing and some textile weaving, while the womenfolk like Mary Wilson knitted by hand the true Fair Isle pullovers – not Shetland or mainland imitations – and each one represented at least forty hours' work. Thelma and I still treasure the pullovers that Mary knitted for us. The island belonged to the National Trust for Scotland and the Master of Works, Alex Warwick, whom I had met on the *Dunera*, soon made himself honorary assistant to the assistant cameraman and helped carry our heavy equipment around the island. We went lobster fishing, filmed birds caught at the Observatory, followed the work on the crofts and captured one sequence of the entire school population – all seven children – on their way to the island school.

Two other films in this series were set on the mainland of Scotland. In the first we shot sequences of an old friend of mine, John Clark, who farmed in Glen Feshie, of red deer with their antlers in velvet boxing each other with their hooves and of the pair of ospreys that were nesting in the forest at Inshriach. One evening I decided to attempt on the following day the ascent of Sgoran Dubh Mor – a 3635-foot-high mountain in the Cairngorms. We would take with us film camera, tripod, magazines and all the other bits and pieces needed for filming. We started the climb at 6 am and moved steadily up through thick mist and cloud until by 9.15 we were just below the 3500-foot contour line. I fixed a camp site where we waited in the mist and I began to wonder if I had chosen the wrong day for the ascent! Then quite without warning at 11.30 am the mist began to lift, streams of light appeared below us and my two companions suddenly realized that I had placed them just above a 2000-foot drop straight down to the dark waters of forbidding Loch Einich – one of the most awesome views in the British Isles. By noon the day was perfect and we gazed across the moss that lay between Sgoran Dubh Mor and the snow-filled corries of Braeriach and Carn Toul. Ptarmigan crackled around us and a line of red deer moved slowly across Coire Odhar. We could see every mountain within a hundred miles. Of the many trips that I have made to the high tops this proved to be one of the finest.

I spent some time in the summer of 1963 at Minsmere, filming with cameraman Geoffrey Mulligan and gathering sequences at this reserve of bitterns, Montagu's and marsh harriers. Here we obtained one of the most remarkable shots of all. But I must go back to 19 May 1952, when I was making sound recordings at Minsmere; on that day I watched two ospreys fishing over the Island Mere. Now in 1963, almost to the very day, I was looking out over the mere once again. 'Let's put up the twenty-four-inch lens on the camera,' I suggested to Geoff. 'You never know but an osprey *might* just turn up!' We both prided ourselves on the speed with which we could have 'Big Bertha', as we called the lens, fitted, with gun-sight, to the camera. Five minutes later – to my utter disbelief – a brown-and-white bird with long narrow wings appeared flying towards us. It was an osprey! 'Run!' I called out. To follow the bird properly in flight Geoff had to manipulate two handles, so that the lens tracked both up and down and from side to side, and he had to keep the focus. The bird never moved away from the centre of his film frame. The osprey circled, hovered and side-slipped down to hit the water, but its quarry – a fish swimming just below the surface – got away. It flapped slowly upwards, gave a quivering shake to rid itself of the water and mounted up to a height of about a hundred feet. Again it plunged downwards without success and once more it climbed up. The camera was running all this time. Once more it dropped down towards the mere and this time it grabbed a fish which it carried headfirst towards our waiting camera and then out of frame. Geoff had held the whole action perfectly. Both Geoffrey Mulligan and Charles Lagus had been with David Attenborough on his *Zoo Quests* and I invited David to deliver the commentaries on this film series. Two years later he became Controller of BBC2 and then later Director of BBC Television. Now he has returned to freelance work.

It had been one of my ambitions to make films with little or no commentary – just first-class sequences, evocatively shot, with good sound recordings of wildlife and atmosphere and a minimum of words. This I was able to do in 1964 when I directed three films, *Dawn, Noon* and *Dusk in the Forest*. There were shots of birds, butterflies, deer, rabbits and hares, moles and bats, and I must have been carrying out as much new wildlife filming at this time in Britain as anyone.

The last major film series in which I was directly involved was *A Year's Journey*. This was an environmental study series intended to stimulate interest in historical and agricultural topics, geography and geology, natural history, land use, transport and communications, local industries and so on. There were twenty-eight films in all. These I presented on the screen and shared the responsibilities of production with my colleague Felicia Elwell. Our journey began in London and moved west to the Isles of Scilly, up the coast of Wales to western Scotland, the Outer Isles, Shetland and then down the east coast to East Anglia. It took us over a year to complete the series which was transmitted on BBC 1 from 1966 to 1967. In 1968 it was decided to remake fourteen of the best films and to add another twenty-eight in colour to provide a complete three-year cycle of films. By this time most children in Britain between the ages of nine and eleven had come to know me by sight.

As I had now been working continuously for seventeen years in radio and television production the Corporation granted me a two months' sabbatical leave to which I was able to add another month's annual leave. My research into woodland birds encouraged me to visit the Irish woodlands. In 1967 the political situation was fairly stable. In fact, the family joined me for a holiday in County Cork. Besides making bird counts, I also had the chance to explore this very beautiful island from the Wicklow Mountains to Galway Bay and from Antrim to remote Mizen Head where I met Anthony Crosland, then Secretary of State for Education and Science whom I had not seen since my Oxford days in 1946. He and his wife were having a brief holiday in County Cork and we discussed education and television.

On my return to the BBC Kenneth Fawdry asked me if I had given any thought to my future in the Corporation, as time was moving on – I was forty-six – and there was a danger, he said, that I might be overtaken by younger and more active producers. Having had the wear and tear of ten years' television work, including many live programmes, I was perhaps looking for a reason to release myself from this particular harness, especially as the natural history output of the department was going down. I said that I would go away and think about it. If I stayed in the BBC to guarantee my pension I foresaw long years of some chairborne, non-productive job and I felt that there was still creative work left in me. There was a risk, if I left, but in the end, with Thelma's total support, I decided to resign. Once I had made up my mind, I slept at night as I had not done for a decade!

15
Dollis Hill

When I started work at the BBC Thelma and I lived for a time with her parents at Dollis Hill in suburban north-west London. My books, specimens and our furniture remained in store while we began the difficult task of finding somewhere to live. Eventually through the help of our good friends, George and Joan Burton, we bought a semi-detached house near the summit of Dollis Hill. The garden of our new home was 180 feet long with shrubs and well-established fruit trees and looked as if it might be a good bird haunt. We could see across the Welsh Harp to Mill Hill and the wooded Stanmore heights.

The area immediately around my house was to become the centre of my natural history attention for the next quarter of a century. Here I was to record 112 different bird species of which thirty bred, although the average number of breeding species fell from twenty-one in 1961 to nineteen in 1971 with growing urbanization. I also noted seventy-nine species in or over my garden and thirteen of these nested, including goldfinch, greenfinch, chaffinch and tree sparrow. The top of Dollis Hill was also a fine vantage point to observe diurnal bird migration taking place, particularly of thrushes, wagtails, swallows, house martins, skylarks, meadow pipits, starlings and chaffinches. I have seen as many as 10 000 starlings and 7500 chaffinches in a single morning. My work on the wildlife of Dollis Hill was to provide material for two scientific papers in the journal *British Birds*, two lectures to the London Natural History Society, including the Hindson Memorial Lecture in 1972, and eventually an important part of my book on the birds of town and suburb for Collins.

Dollis Hill

Dollis Hill has become quite well known as a result of my radio and television programmes about its natural history. It, of course, adjoins Neasden, which has for so long been the butt of *Private Eye* and which has gained fame or notoriety, according to where *you* live, quite out of proportion to its size or charm. Jack de Manio interviewed me about the wildlife of Neasden in his programme *Jack de Manio Precisely* and shortly afterwards I took *The Living World* team of presenter Derek Jones, producer Dilys Breese and assistant Sue Coates for a guided tour of my study area for their Radio 4 programme on Sundays. We listened to the dawn chorus, visited Gladstone Park, the Brook Road allotments and the Welsh Harp, which although a shadow of its former self is still worthy of conservation for its wildlife. In 1972 Edward Mirzoeff produced a delightful film in which Sir John Betjeman took a journey through Metroland out from Baker Street to darkest Buckinghamshire. He found homes of lust and mystery in St John's Wood, my nature trail in Neasden, the Great Tower of London in Wembley, midsummer revels in Croxley Green and a mighty Wurlitzer in Chorleywood. Having been a devotee of the Metropolitan Railway, this was a delightful film to be associated with. *The Times* reported that 'Mr Eric Simms took us on the Neasden Nature Trail, through the glades of Gladstone Park and up to the allotments of Brook Road. "There's such a good view from the top that I can pick up birds at a great distance," he told us, and Sir John Betjeman nodded gravely.'

Both Thelma and I became busy with local activities – for her the Townswomen's Guild and the Willesden Society – while I lectured to local organizations and opened exhibitions in addition to my provincial and national lecturing. But our home and happiness were incomplete. When it became clear that we were not going to have any children of our own we decided to try to adopt some. With the support of Leonard Marre, our family doctor and brother of the Ombudsman, Sir Alan Marre, we approached an adoption society known for its stringent and exacting rules to protect the children in their care. After a number of interviews and other formalities we were accepted and went off to celebrate in Switzerland. Our base was a pleasant pension some 2000 feet above Lake Geneva near the village of Chardonne, and on the wooded slopes of Mont Pèlerin. From our bedroom window we looked down on terraced vineyards falling steeply away towards Charlie Chaplin's house and English-style garden and the town of Vevey. Across the lake towered the snowy summits of Grammont, the Dent d'Oche and Les Dents du Midi. East of the valley rose the canine fang of Jaman and higher still the precipitous ridges of Les Rochers de Naye. The whole scene was one of superb and uplifting grandeur. The pension garden was gay with roses, pinks, foxgloves, cacti and prickly pears, while the apple and cherry trees were full of the songs of redstarts, serins and Bonelli's warblers.

I was away filming in South Wales when Thelma telephoned me to say that we could collect our infant son, aged three weeks. After an anxious period we finally appeared nine months later in front of His Honour H. C. Leon – county court judge but better known as Henry Cecil, author and playwright. He signed the order which made David Barford our legal son. Both Thelma and I thought it would be wrong to have only one adopted child and so in 1962 Judge Leon signed a second order by which Amanda Jane became our daughter. Life with a young family was now full and complete. We could only wish our children happiness in their lives and that they would be content in the home in which they found themselves.

The children have experienced the usual childish ailments but I do recall the autumn of 1965 when David had his tonsils removed. This took place at the same time as another boy patient explained to his mother that 'it was God who operated on me'. The boy said, 'When I went into the big room, there were two lady angels all dressed in white. Then two men angels came in. One of the men angels looked down my throat and said, "God! Look at that child's tonsils!" and God looked and said, "I'll take them out at once!"'

We spent our early family holidays in our beloved Aberdeenshire to which Thelma's parents moved to be near their other daughter Jeanne. Here there were sandy beaches, rocky coves and heather moors to explore and both children developed a strong affection for this part of Scotland, now so hard-pressed by industrialization. We had holidays too at Dunster in

Somerset where I was able to carry out regular migration watches along the Bristol Channel.

As the children grew we began to travel more. We spent family holidays at Nefyn in North Wales and Schull in County Cork, but we moved further afield to widen their experience. We visited Italy as far east as Venice, we travelled in Provence to see the Roman antiquities as well as the egrets and flamingoes of the Camargue, and we explored the alpine heights of the Bernese Oberland. One of our favourite haunts has been Arosa in the Grisons. It is a comparatively isolated town on the River Plessur and is encompassed by mountains that rise to 8000 feet and more. Arosa lies snugly at 5000 feet above sea level among belts of conifers rich in orchids, alpine plants, butterflies, shy roedeer and black-phase red squirrels which used to feed out of the children's hands. The canopy of the woodland was alive with the whispered calls of coal, great and European crested tits which were also tame enough to feed from the hand. Above the treeline were hay meadows full of campanulas, rampions, vetches and more orchids while rhododendrons, primulas, saxifrages and stemless gentians blossomed on the higher alpine slopes. At 8000 feet where the snow-beds melt and retreat we found the hanging violet-blue funnels of the alpine snowbell – the soldanella. Here among the snow-beds and on the eroded screes were cushions of rose-coloured moss campion, the white heads of pasque flowers and mountain avens, golden-yellow mountain buttercups, pale saxifrages and crucifers, purple milk vetches and primulas and the sky-blue 'King of the Alps' – *Eritrichium nanum.*

These flowering high-altitude meadows are one of Nature's greatest spectacles. We saw quite a few ravens, crows, wheatears, water pipits, blue rock thrushes and occasionally a golden eagle. At the higher levels were snow finches, alpine accentors and alpine choughs; at Malbun in Liechtenstein families of choughs used to come down and meet us for titbits. Three mammals are especially associated with these high alpine meadows. One is the sure-footed chamois which I saw on the higher slopes of the Schiesshorn and the second is the alpine marmot. Many times we saw marmots sitting up on their hind legs feeding on some small delicacy held between their front paws or lolloping up a sunny slope. Others just sunbathed on the warm rocks or chased each other in a sportive way. If they scented danger they gave a series of short bird-like whistles. These marmots spend the winter, which can last from six to eight months, hibernating in deep burrows under the snow and they seemed determined to enjoy their short summer to the full! Early one morning we were near the summit of the Weisshorn where we were rewarded with superb views of two adult ibex and a playful kid. We once stalked a single male as he ran across a meadow near the summit of the Hörnli. These fine views of a rare European mammal moving wild and free among the snows and mists of the high Alps were part of the attraction that led us as a family back to Switzerland.

On 23 February 1965 I was sworn in at Middlesex Sessions by Judge J. A. Grieves as a Justice of the Peace for the Petty Sessional Division of Willesden – one of the eight divisions for Greater London. The work of the magistrates' courts fell into two broad categories – civil, which dealt with adoption, matrimonial matters and so on, and criminal, which was much the larger of the two. A summary trial had to be before a petty sessional court and Number One Court at Willesden must have been one of the busiest lay courts in the country.

A typical morning for me might begin by my hearing applications for summonses at ten o'clock and then going to sit with other magistrates at half past ten in one of the courts. Number One Court might deal with applications for remands and 'ordinary' crime, while the others might take a list of motoring offences or a few cases likely to take a long time. Many prosecutions were conducted by a police inspector, but solicitors and barristers had a right of audience. On a number of occasions Sir Learie (later Lord) Constantine appeared before me to present the case for the prosecution and I shall always remember his unfailing courtesy, fairness and patience.

There was a general right of appeal from petty sessions to Middlesex Area Sessions – now the Crown Court – and some cases had to be committed for trial there, including those in which the accused claimed his right to trial by jury. Cases for trial were always heard in the first instance in the magistrates' court where the magistrates sat not as judges but as 'examining justices'. I have sometimes sat all day alone, since this function could be performed by a single magistrate. All county justices were entitled to sit at courts of quarter sessions and I regularly sat as a judge with the chairman or deputy chairman in Middlesex Guildhall on a trial of an indictable case which had been committed to the sessions by examining justices. When I first attended at the Middlesex Guildhall the Chairman was the Hon. Ewen Montagu, QC, Judge Advocate of the Fleet and author of *The Man Who Never Was*. He expressed the view on his retirement in 1969 that he had dealt with more offenders on indictable charges than any other judge in England. I found it both a stirring and humbling experience to sit as a judge at sessions where Sir George Jeffreys and author Henry Fielding had preceded me on the bench and in whose dock had stood such figures as Sir Walter Raleigh, Daniel Defoe and Christopher Marlowe.

16

African Safari

As a young boy I had always been fascinated by Africa. I met Emil Torday – a great explorer who had traversed the wildernesses of the Belgian Congo; his widow went on holiday to Belgium with my mother in the late 1930s. Colonel Meinertzhagen had delighted me with stories of rhinoceroses in the outskirts of Nairobi and of his exciting quest for the giant forest hog that bears his name. Yes! I had read Selous and I also knew about the man-eaters of Tsavo. In 1965 our two children were still quite young and able to spend Christmas in Scotland with Jeanne and her husband Lewis Gordon. The political situation in Africa was becoming increasingly uncertain and so Thelma and I agreed that it would be unwise to delay a safari to 'the dark continent' much longer. It was organized through Hotelplan of Switzerland and our party was to consist of seven travellers; the other members were a young Englishman – Peter Northey who had just left Wellington College, and is now a professional photographer, Dr Karl Käfer of Zürich University and his wife Hermi, and M. and Mme Pierre André. Pierre was the Head of the Secretariat of the European Parliament.

We left Zürich in a Britannia on 20 December 1965, climbing steadily over the Alps and setting course down the leg of Italy for the Mediterranean. We flew over the African coast near Benghazi and turned south-east across the Sahara Desert. For hour after hour a tawny landscape unfolded beneath us – without trees, rivers or lakes and ridged with ripples, cracks and sandy slopes many feet high. Sand storms twisted and whirled across the surface of the desert. For more than a thousand miles we travelled over a great brown emptiness.

We reached the Nile at Aswan, circled the Fourth Cataract and, following the strip of cultivated land along the river, set off for Khartoum. From the window Thelma and I could see the junction of the White and Blue Niles, Omdurman and rows and rows of buildings in Kitchener's city laid out in military review order. We landed on the sandy runway at Khartoum and, as we emerged stiff and sore, the heat was savage, beating like a muffled sledgehammer on the brain. Tall Sudanese served lemonade. There were Sudan house sparrows on the roof of the airport and black kites swooping and playing among the parked aircraft. An African white wagtail ran across the grass in front of the transit lounge where it called more sharply and emphatically than its European counterpart.

On the next stage of our flight we could see the 170-mile-long strip of Lake Rudolph with its giant crocodiles and we crossed the Equator at about 36°30' west. For several minutes we glimpsed above the towering cumulus clouds the great volcanic plug of Mount Kenya, jagged, impassive and laced with narrow beds of snow in its high corries. As we approached Nairobi, a softer, more cultivated landscape began to appear. At the airport we were greeted by a black-and-white fiscal shrike and a gaudy starling. Here we collected a Volkswagen minibus and its tall Somali driver – Hussein Ega – with a fine sense of humour and occasion, and at least seven years' valuable service with the British Army.

Nairobi itself was graced with broad avenues gay with blue jacarandas, red hibiscus and crimson bougainvillaea and was aglow with a tropical evening light. There were tall euphorbias and squat grey bayonet aloes growing on the roundabouts in Uhuru Highway and at the road junctions. Black kites and pied crows were flying along the road verges where countless butterflies and black-and-white hummingbird hawk-moths winked and hovered. Then we were off on the road to Nakuru. By now it was dark and a slow-moving aard-vaark – a rare sight indeed – wandered across the highway near Lake Naivasha. We were soon in the Stag's Head Hotel at Nakuru where we could hear the shrill crickets in the street. We also had a good look at their well-stocked bird room.

I was up early next morning watching the variable and

amethyst sunbirds in the garden – tiny, sickle-billed gems of mauve and blue feeding among the flowers. After an early breakfast we took a narrow dirt road where European swallows drifted around us and parties of nimble sinewy impala turned to stare at us. We drove round a small rubbish dump with its three attendant marabou storks and there it was! – perhaps the greatest ornithological sight on earth. A thin dazzling line of rose-pink forms stretched away along the shore of a shallow lake for thousands of yards. Hussein drove to the edge of Lake Nakuru and we climbed out. The air was clean and dry, and the pollution, which we were to hear so much about later on, was not very apparent. As we walked very slowly along the edge of the lake myriads of greater and lesser flamingoes retreated slowly on their long legs to a distance of only twenty yards from the shore.

'*Formidable!*' exclaimed Pierre André.

There were at least one and a half million lesser flamingoes, some waving their black-and-crimson banners, others slowly beating their way over the soda-impregnated lake. The fresh African morning was full of goose-like honks and trumpetings. Dividing us from the solid phalanx of the flamingoes, when we had recovered enough to look around, were groups of black-winged stilts, little stints from the Arctic, marsh sandpipers from the Russian steppes and resident blacksmith plovers and Kittlitz's sand plovers. Two sacred ibises strolled purposefully along the shore and by the water's edge were herons, little egrets and a few pelicans. Through my field glasses I could see little grebes, darters, southern pochard and cape wigeon on the surface of Nakuru. Nearby on a clod of earth was a common wheatear – a migrant from the north. Nakuru was a great experience and a marvellous opening to our African journey.

The next stage of our safari was to take us to Paraa and the Murchison Falls Park, now renamed the Kabalega National Park. North-west of Nakuru, Peter Northey quietly remarked, as we passed some scrubby grassland, 'I think they must be giraffe!'

'Where?' I asked.

'There! Among those trees!' And there they were, reaching up and pulling off thin branches with their long tongues. From now on we began to see a whole host of birds of prey, including a fine martial eagle, several narrow-winged Wahlberg's eagles, black-chested harrier eagles and quite a few Bateleur eagles with their characteristically short tails. Along the sides of the roads were eroded cones of red earth, some ten feet high or more, which were the vast engineering works of the termites. Many of the earthbanks showed the severe scouring effect of the rainy season. We recrossed the equator at 9000 feet and the next bird species to add to my African list, believe it or not, was a moorhen!

After crossing the frontier into Uganda we stopped at the Rock Hotel at Tororo. This was very pleasantly situated among wide lawns bordered with flower-beds and here Peter Northey and I looked at the butterflies. Some were black-and-white with polka dots, others were honey-brown, blue or yellow, and all were dancing and hovering above the lines of petunias. Grey-headed sparrows were sitting about in the bushes, chattering conversationally or gathering nest material. On the telegraph wires sat a pair of swallows so gaily-coloured that I could hardly believe that they were real. These were striped swallows with rufous-chestnut crowns and rumps and black streaks down their chests. Their metallic calls were mingled with brief warbles; they were the oddest swallows that I had ever seen.

We saw our first cattle egrets at Jinja and these were actually in attendance, not on big game, but on cattle. Thelma and I went and stood by the Owen Falls where a huge spout of water gushed out from the great crescent of a concrete dam. For both of us this was quite a moment, for under the turmoil of waters was the spot where on 28 July 1862 John Hanning Speke discovered the source of the Nile. 'It was', he said, 'a sight that attracted me for hours – the roar of the waters . . . hippopotamus and crocodiles lying sleepily on the waters.' Swarms of African sand martins circled above the water, while lines of white-necked cormorants and darters made their two-way passage over the Nile. At this point Lake Victoria lay due south, Lake Kioga due north.

From the capital Kampala the road to Paraa ran north – a dusty red strip of bumps and corrugations. For the first time we began to see palms in numbers, including the tall Borassus palm which can be recognized by its orange-yellow fruits and a stem which swells in the middle like a chair spar. There were also cactus-like euphorbias shaped into giant candelabras. We reached Masindi, once the capital of the Bunyoro Kingdom of Kabarega. A saddle-billed stork was soaring on broad pinions overhead and a red-eyed dove sang a high, monotonous 'Koo-koo-koo . . . koo-koo-koo'. As Thelma was the first to locate the singer after Peter and I had signally failed, we called the species 'Thelma's dove' from then on.

We entered the Murchison Falls Park near the River Waiga and, sitting on a dead tree, was the first of the many African fish eagles that we would see. This is a wild country depopulated by the tsetse-fly and sleeping sickness. The Volkswagen was moving towards a group of trees – I think they were terminalia – when we spotted our first herd of elephants. There were nine of them standing with slowly flapping ears and coiling and uncoiling trunks, stuffing themselves with some of the hundred pounds of vegetable matter that they need each day. Somehow these first elephants, most of which were adult, looked rather small, set in their natural savannah landscape. Shortly afterwards we came across thirteen more browsing along a lush, watery stream and this time the nearest animal was close enough to convey something of its great majesty and size. Of course, these big pachyderms need to be seen in their natural habitat. Two old bulls that we approached did not condescend to give us even a glance. We really felt insignificant – tiny visitors lost in the world of the Pleistocene.

The park was full of tall grass grown during the recent rains. Over these great plains roamed tall Jackson's hartebeest, standing fifty inches at the shoulder and with long V-shaped horns the tips of which pointed directly backwards. There were smaller red-gold Uganda kob with lyre-shaped horns that had been adopted as the emblem of the Uganda National Parks. And there were graceful oribi – small antelopes with long necks. We saw several herds of buffalo and one group of 250 animals spread in a long broad line across the savannah. We caught one buffalo in his mud wallow and he made off with a thunder of hooves. A warthog with tail up like a periscope streaked away towards his home in a termite heap. Pallid and

Montagu's harriers quartered the grasslands looking for small prey and two ground hornbills stalked over the plain like black turkeys. In the distance a column of white-grey smoke revealed the start of a fire, something that we were to see a number of times in Uganda. Then the road ran straight down to the Nile. We waited under a desert date for the ferry to take us across the river to Paraa. Fish eagles laughed all the way down the broad stream, Egyptian geese honked overhead and hadada ibises bleated and brayed from the opposite bank.

Here was the Nile – the second mightiest river on earth, embellished by our memories of Bible readings and our knowledge of Ancient Egypt – and we were actually standing by it! Three hippos grunted rhythmically in midstream and in the lush riverside vegetation were an old buffalo and a bull elephant. On the far side I could see a kigelia, or sausage tree, ornamented with three-foot-long fruits, hanging down on long stalks. As the ferry made its way across the brown waters of the Nile, a malachite kingfisher drew a brilliant blue line above the stream. Our base at Paraa was a comfortable bungalow with a verandah; here on the parapet was a hideous eighteen-inch-long reptile, crudely coloured with a blood-orange head and tail and a blue-grey body and looking as if it had been run over by a car. It was bobbing up and down in a most menacing fashion. Then with legs apparently worked by a spring it moved in an obscene, primeval way up the wall and settled itself in the sun above our heads. The agama – for such it was – was one of the least prepossessing animals that I had ever come across. All the time we could hear the heavy spoutings and gruntings of the hippos below our front door, as they slowly surfaced and submerged. Lily trotters with chestnut backs and big feet crept over the waterside vegetation. A marabou stork flew in to roost in a nearby tree. And in equatorial Africa night falls very quickly indeed.

After our evening meal Peter Northey, Thelma and I sat outside the lodge which had been opened by Sir Peter Scott some years before. Our seats were in the penumbra of a bank of lights which brilliantly illuminated some refuse bunkers at the rear of the lodge. That night two adult elephants and a calf came to the scraps of food. One of the adults then began to browse forward, passing through the barrier of the lights towards us, tearing branches from a tree and disturbing clouds of yellow-winged bats. So close did he come that even in the darkness I could see every wrinkle on his trunk, every flute in the ivory of his tusks. Still he came forward and when he had less than twelve feet to go to reach us our courage failed and we hastily withdrew. At the sudden scuffle he turned away and moved back into the shelter of the night. A few minutes later the other elephants drifted away. A bush genet ran across the area of light and then three spotted hyaenas – ugly and suspicious – slunk up to feed. A hyaena had shown up earlier but it was soon put to flight by a sharp trumpet from the cow elephant. We could see the hyaenas' sloping backs, acquired, according to local legend, from carrying witches around on them. The spots on their flanks showed up quite clearly. From time to time they turned round ears and large wet noses in our direction.

By half past eleven all was quiet at the lodge and we walked back to our bungalow. There – to our astonishment – across the entrance to the verandah was a full grown hippopotamus, broad and fat and quietly munching away at the dry, sandy grass. At first it refused to move and I was taking no chances. The hippo can be a far more speedy and dangerous animal than many people care to believe. It has been known to bite a man in two, so I made sure that Thelma and I did not get between it and the Nile. By directing the full beam of my torch into its eyes, I finally persuaded it to move, somewhat reluctantly, far enough away for us to make a quick dash for the bungalow door. All that night with two companions it munched its way round our refuge, blowing occasionally and with loud rumbling noises escaping from its stomach. Often it was less than three feet from our open netted window.

The next day was our wedding anniversary and I woke to hear the clear warblings of a red-backed scrub robin. Again the morning was fresh and sharp – I was not yet conditioned to the fact that every morning would rise cloudless and full of promise. As soon as it was light I explored an erosion gully above the river. An acrid smell of hippo droppings filled the narrow sandy defile which was obviously a route up from the river. Translucent brownish pebbles of quartzite glowed and refracted the rays of the rising sun. Within five minutes I had found a chipped pebble tool – a sign that prehistoric man had also found this a good camp site.

After breakfast we chugged our way in a launch up the Nile and in the direction of the Murchison Falls. A European common sandpiper peeped from a sandbank, tall solitary goliath herons and white egrets fished in some of the shallow bays and every few yards the expected fish eagle sat on a stag-headed riverside tree, sometimes throwing back a head and cackling loudly. All round us great heads and backs heaved in the water with mighty blowings and sighings as the hippos rose and fell. One animal was out on the bank and I photographed him; another had a huge red gash across the hindquarters, caused perhaps by the formidable tushes of another hippo or by the claws of a marauding lion. Crocodiles were lying on the banks and mudflats, some looking like river driftwood, others with their hideous mouths agape. This stretch of the River Nile is one of the best places in the world to see these great reptiles. As we came to within ten to fifteen yards the crocodiles would suddenly haul up on to their short legs and with a strange mechanical waddle make for the river where they slid easily into the bubbling, beer-brown water. Those who left their withdrawal to the last moment entered the protecting river with a tremendous splash. One giant crocodile of great age had its own special entourage of water dikkops, green-backed herons and a little black crake with coral-red legs and bill and yellow frontal shield. We also saw quite a number of Nile monitors – lizards up to six feet long which preyed on the crocodiles' eggs. Nearby a black openbill stork and a wood ibis were contemplating their reflections in a shallow pool. On branches above the river sat pied kingfishers, wire-tailed swallows and – most brilliant of all – groups of lovely carmine bee-eaters.

An elephant came down to the water's edge to drink and then tug up great hunks of grass. Eight waterbuck with thick greyish-brown coats and heavily ringed, backward- and-outward-curving horns were browsing in a clearing and a family of baboons cantered along the river-bank. As we rounded a bend in the river we began to see froth drifting past the launch. I looked ahead at the same moment as Thelma exclaimed 'There it is!' In front of us, in the distance, was a white triangle of spray and spume that revealed the Murchison Falls themselves. It was now very hot indeed – the air was stifling and our vision reeled and swam as we looked across to the glowing furnace that was the bank. A fine lion, disturbed by our approach, tried to drag its kill – a hippo – up the slope. As we drifted in more closely, with the engine cut, he snarled at us, moved up the bank and hid himself behind a bush. Paraa – 'the place of the hippos' – was really living up to its name.

The falls themselves were discovered in March 1864 by Samuel Baker and his wife, both ill at the time and near the limits of their endurance. Here the broad waters of the Nile crash down some 140 feet through a rock gap only nineteen feet wide. A deluge in 1961 created two smaller falls alongside the original one, but these had not diminished the grandeur of the spectacle. We stood on another day by the very edge of these falls, peering down into the great cascade of boiling white water. On a wave-washed boulder in the middle of the foaming torrent I spotted three of the rare white-collared pratincoles. This great natural wonder of the world and the park fell under the threat at a later time of a hydro-electric scheme, first proposed in 1969, but after an outcry among conservationists this plan was cancelled in September 1971 by President Idi Amin.

In many ways Paraa was the highlight of our safari. From this superb reserve we drove to Masindi, passing countless numbers of elephants, buffalo and impala and having fine views of the blue and grey woodland kingfisher and the blue-eared glossy starling. After a night in Masindi we journeyed on to the Karuma Falls. Here the Victoria Nile roars through rocky rapids, round tiny islands crowned with scrub and then plunges at forty miles an hour over a rock step below the bridge. For an hour we watched the tumbling river with swallows and martins dipping over the road and white-backed vultures circling on rectangular wings high in the air. The sun was hot, but the closeness of the Nile and its cascades of water gave the atmosphere a fresh clean quality. In a backwater, not far from the spot where Mrs Samuel Baker had washed her waist-long yellow hair to the consternation of Kamrasi's tribesmen, three African youths were laundering their clothes and, after laying them out on the rocks to dry in the sun, took their own ablutions in the stream. It was an idyllic scene. Since our visit reports suggest that the Nile here has been used for more sinister purposes.

In one Ugandan village, where the children's faces had a remarkable symmetry and beauty, a festive bullock was being divided up under the village council tree with a felling axe. The dusty African air, laden with a pungent smell of putridity, was full of patient circling African black kites. We camped in a clearing near the shore of Lake Kioga under some acacias and the villagers came out to entertain us quite spontaneously, but the dance that they chose for us was the twist with musical accompaniment from a tuneful xylophone of local design.

From Kachung the road turned right to Soroti and it was full of villagers passing each other like two lines of ants coming and going on the same foraging route from their nest. Lime-green dresses – the colour of a bright, ubiquitous little butterfly – especially flattered the dark-skinned Ugandan women. They carried all their burdens on their heads in a quite imperial manner – baskets of fruit or groceries, flat bowls, petrol cans full of water, pieces of wood, clothes, and, on one occasion, just a small box of matches cleverly balanced on a tiny cube of soap! The red dust from the road had been splashed up by the recent rains leaving an orange skirt along the mud-huts almost two feet high. In the watery central area of Uganda we saw stemless palms, papyrus swamps and lagoons starred with blue water-lillies where glossy ibises and openbill storks were common. We finally reached Mbale and drove into the cool, flowery gardens of the Mount Elgon Hotel where the noise from the singing crickets and cicadas was almost unbearable.

A safari such as ours had involved long drives in considerable heat and dust and it was soon clear that it requires a certain stamina to travel through Africa. We were glad to relax at the Tea Hotel in Kericho. We sat in the garden, after meals fit for the gods, and enjoyed the jacarandas and bottle-brush trees, the soft springy lawns, the fountain and the goldfish pool. It was a most restful spot with a white-browed robin chat in song and half a dozen European bee-eaters flying and calling over the grass.

Fully refreshed, we now took the road through the tea-lands of Sotik to the Masai Mara Game Reserve. We met our first Masai warriors with red-ochred plaits, pierced ears and red-brown togas. They were guarding some bony-looking cattle and goats with fearsome-looking spears; these had two-inch-wide blades with parallel sides about three feet long. They were quite capable of killing a rhinoceros with a single blow. The Masai warriors were very tall and thin with slender hips. Two maidens, unshaven spinsters gaily decked out with rows of beads and copper ear-rings and carrying gourds, tried to win a lift from us, but Hussein's remarks in Swahili soon had them laughing at their disappointment. We stopped to have lunch at Keekorok Lodge – a modern Swedish-style safari centre which had been opened by Jomo Kenyatta not long before our visit. Vervet monkeys were playing around the trees, a large buffalo was dozing the day away under an acacia and all round the lodge termites were raising their six-inch-high cooling towers in the earth.

From Keekorok the route turned south towards the Serengeti Plains and Tanzania. In the scrubby country near Klein's Camp, where eyeless buffalo skulls stared up at us from the ground, we saw considerable numbers of buffalo, warthogs, impala, topi, helmeted guinea-fowl and our first cheetah. From the bush we ran out on to mile after mile of grassy plain where zebras, looking like dusty grey ponies, and top-heavy wildebeest were roaming in their thousands. Many of them were grazing near the road and only moved at the last minute. There were herds of Thomson's gazelles – red-brown with black lateral stripes and affectionately known as 'Tommies' – kongonis, topi and a single large eland. Jackals trotted across the grasslands and Kori bustards stalked majestically over the savannahs – dominating birds whose imperious and detached appearance quickly endeared them to Thelma and myself. I was also very pleased to see numbers of white storks and secretary birds pacing over the grass on long legs while they hunted for grasshoppers.

The great plains of the Serengeti National Park unwound themselves like some strange parkland with flat green acacias to break the tawny monotony. Then the trees began to thicken, the road curved round a clump of forest trees and there in front of us was a kopje, or inselberg, formed from huge granite slabs and boulders, some with rounded edges, others split into rocky biscuits and all fashioned by chemical and thermal wear. A few native huts clustered round the foot of the kopje behind a half-completed wooden fence of tall stakes. Small bushes clung to the rocky slopes and, silhouetted against the rosy evening sky on the highest pinnacle, was the tiny figure of a rock hyrax – the nearest living relative of the mighty elephant. Fan-tailed ravens croaked among the rocks, and superb starlings whistled and grey-headed social weavers moved fussily around an umbrella acacia. This was Seronera Camp.

We sat drinking coffee by a huge fire in the open African night. Above us shone the brilliance of the Southern Cross and Orion lying back to front rather than up and down. As we lay in our mosquito nets we could hear the weird rising howls of hyaenas and the distant roar of lions. The Serengeti is especially renowned for its lions and on the next morning we found a lioness, deeply engrossed, stalking slowly but purposefully a wildebeest standing looking at her some 400 yards away. Like a great tawny pussy-cat the lioness moved forward in slow motion, then she paused before moving on again – and the wildebeest never once took its eyes off the big cat. There were many fine black-maned lions and one of their favourite haunts used to be in the shadow of a rock at the foot of a kopje. Many of the lionesses preferred to sleep on the very highest slabs of the rocky piles. On one expedition we came across a pride of five lionesses lying in the short grass and about to go hunting.

On our drive back to camp we stopped to chat to an English family who had not seen a single lion in a whole week of travelling in the reserves. Shortly after this encounter we flushed three cheetahs from the grass, and Hussein, committing himself to a cross-country scramble, set off in pursuit of one of them. For five minutes we twisted, swerved and bulldozed our way across a brown sea of grass, over ridges and burrows, through defiles and around swampy depressions and termite hills in hot pursuit. I glanced at the speedometer, and the cheetah, for which we were putting our limbs, perhaps our lives, in peril, could not manage more than 45 mph. It checked, changed direction, sprinted, slowed and tore away again in great bounds, and then, quite suddenly, as if its engine had been turned off, it threw itself down on the ground with heaving flanks in total submission. After getting its breath back it walked off rather slowly into the savannah.

The Serengeti Plains were fascinating. Topi – sturdy antelopes with brown and purple markings and looking like skinned rabbits – were standing high on vantage points provided by eroded termite nests. There were vast numbers of zebra and wildebeest, and sprightly little 'Tommies'. We saw small herds of Grant's gazelles, which were superbly graceful animals with dark-bordered white rumps and fine lyre-shaped horns. We also watched reedbuck and tiny foot-high dik-diks – miniature antelopes with legs like pencils. I was busy checking on all the birds in the short grass from ostriches, storks and secretary birds down to Caspian plovers, crowned lapwings, coursers, spurfowl, ruffs, Richard's pipits, red-capped and flappet larks.

At Seronera was a rushy pool which attracted egrets, marabou storks and wading birds, including greenshanks and wood sandpipers. Hooded vultures sat in the trees and a leopard had his lair among the rocks, coming down to drink at the pool. The villagers invited Thelma and me to watch them calling down the hyraxes from the kopje to be fed with titbits. They weighed a couple of pounds each and came so close to us that we could see their sharp bewhiskered faces and the horny pads on their feet which help them in climbing the rocks. One night I persuaded Thelma to come with me to the village refuse pit. I shone my torch across the dump. Less than fifteen yards away four pairs of liquid green eyes suddenly glowed as they turned towards us. We froze where we stood. Suddenly the nearest pair of lamps was reduced momentarily to one as a hyaena blinked one eye! Six months later we read Dr Hans Kruuk's article in the *New Scientist* entitled 'A New View of the Hyaena' in which he described the animal as a skilful and resourceful hunter in his own right, so dispelling the conventional picture of the hyaena as nothing but a mean fearful scavenger.

One of the most spectacular wildlife haunts in the world is the Ngorongoro Crater – a caldera covering more than a hundred square miles and lying to the south-east of Seronera. To reach it we travelled across the southern part of the Serengeti National Park. Giraffe with the attractive patterns of the Masai race wandered across the dirt road. Ostriches appeared in scattered groups and four eland, moving at about 40 mph, crossed diagonally in front of us. Hundreds of wildebeest, zebra and Thomson's gazelles played 'last across', dashing at breakneck speed from one side of the track to the other. The huge ungainly wildebeest made awkward right-angle swerves with the rudders of their tails fully stretched out and their hooves biting into the dry ground with little puffs of dust exploding from the earth. We stopped to look at a pride of seven lionesses hunting zebra. White storks were everywhere and great coveys of dove-like sand-grouse rose up from the roadside.

The Volkswagen now started to climb out of the plains and we began to see groups of whistling thorns decorated with plum-sized black galls, each containing an ant colony. As a breeze passes the entrance holes, the galls 'sing'. Pink amaryllises blossomed in splendid isolation among the grass and rushes growing on the slopes of the Crater Highlands. At a height of 8000 feet we found large cabbage-like groundsels and giant lobelias with eight-foot-tall spikes of flowers. As the air grew thinner the older members of our party began to feel unwell and I opened up my medicine chest.

From our headquarters on the volcano's lip we looked down some 2000 feet on to a twelve-mile-wide plain – mainly grassland, but with patches of dense acacia forest and brackish lakes and swamps. The Olduvai Gorge is not far away and, as Dr Louis Leakey had been filmed shaping flint tools in my office in the BBC's Kensington House, I was sorry not to have had time to visit it. To reach the bottom of the Ngorongoro Crater we travelled in a Land-Rover in four-wheel drive under the control of an African ranger. The route, known as the

Lerai Descent, was a perilously steep and winding track down the slopes of the crater wall. There were big herds of wildebeest, Burchell's zebra, kongonis, Grant's and Thomson's gazelles feeding on the grassland which seemed fairly rich in small clovers. A Verreaux's eagle was circling overhead, an Egyptian vulture was sitting on a clod of earth and European wheatears were using the whitened skulls of long-dead animals as perches. We climbed out at the lakeside to survey the shallow stretch of water. A few hippos grunted and blew far out on the crater lake. Greater flamingoes stalked through the shallows, while through my field glasses I also spotted great crested grebes, maccoa and yellow-billed ducks, European shoveler, African pochard and red-knobbed coot. Tawny eagles were flying over the mudbanks. There were many hyaenas sitting about at their burrows and both black-backed and golden jackals were trotting across the dry earth. Two lions were guarding their kill in a grassy clump, while thirty yards away in a half-crescent sat a group of waiting jackals and white-backed vultures. And then came a moment that we had been awaiting since we first arrived in East Africa. In front of us was an ashy-white black rhinoceros that had just come from his favourite mud wallow which had left him pale and most interesting.

On our trek across the crater floor we witnessed a strange anomalous sight – a pair of ruined walls, six feet high and built of stone, quite unlike the mud huts of the Masai. The tumbled-down stones were partly hidden by some bushes on a slight hill which was dominated by a tall Australian eucalyptus or gumtree. This used to be the home of a German settler called Adolf Seidentopf, who, in the early part of this century, with his brother kept some 1200 head of cattle here as well as breeding ostriches and trying to tame zebras, which pulled well enough but did not have the staying power of horses. The brothers Seidentopf also organized lion hunts on the grand scale, but they were forced to leave when the British took over German East Africa after the First World War. We lunched among the ruins and relieved nature with some trepidation, keeping a weather eye open for leopards and any of the crater's 400 lions.

Back once more in the Land-Rover, we went in search of more rhinos and actually approached to within twelve feet of two adults standing dozing in the sun. Not far away was a cow rhino with a little twelve-month-old baby. We revisited the lake where butterflies and grasshoppers were common. There were grey-headed gulls, sacred ibis and an African spoonbill. In the forest strip near the exit road we came across three elephants, several buffaloes and a number of waterbuck. There were a few baboons about and groups of ostriches which made off with their round bodies rolling from side to side. On one muddy pool there were 400 migrant little stints.

At night leopards and buffaloes used to wander past our wooden chalet on the crater edge, leaving their pugmarks and prints in the small flower-bed outside the front door. I was always out in the early morning looking for golden-winged sunbirds in the scrub with its yellow pea-like flowers. In this way I found a lying-up place for an old male buffalo and a sheltered glade where two shy bushbuck came out to feed. Here I talked to a young Masai as a leopard, hidden up in a deep rainwater gully, watched us from barely thirty feet. The leopard also used to make his way along a track on the journey back to his lair. We saw him cross two clearings on his dawn travels and once we watched a dog following up the trail of this handsome and dangerous cat.

We left Ngorongoro with regret. It had proved exactly what Dr Bernhard Grzimek – the author of *Serengeti Shall Not Die* – had called it: 'the largest zoo in the world'. Our descent to the south from the crater rim was a hazardous one. As we neared the end of our steep drop towards the Oldeani–Arusha road, an ominous and rhythmic clonk began to emanate from the front of the minibus. I lay on the ground while Hussein inched the vehicle forward. 'Stop!' I shouted as the sound began again, less regular and lower in pitch. I levered off a hubcap and three hot bolts fell out! The two remaining wheel bolts needed only a half-turn and a full turn for them to drop out.

There were quite a few elephants and buffalo in the ground-water forest by Lake Manyara, with its great fig and mahogany trees and tree-climbing lions. On the road between Makuyuni and Arusha we were thrilled to see our first baobabs – upside-down trees with soft bloated trunks and short thick branches. The landscape was an arid one, with extensive and very thick thorn brakes. Here for the first time we saw fringe-eared oryx and those extraordinary long-legged and giraffe-necked antelopes – gerenuks. While we were filling up with petrol in Arusha a predatory species of fly ran a white-hot dagger into my neck and retreated out through the sun roof before I could take retaliatory action. The pain was excruciating and the subsequent aches and stomach cramps rather spoilt my run to Namanga. Hussein put his foot down and drove at top speed across the grey volcanic dust of a dried-up lake towards Ol Tukai in the Amboseli Masai Game Reserve.

At half past six the next morning we went out to see the sun rise on Kilimanjaro. The great 19 000-foot snow cone of Kibo was clear of cloud – ice-blue in the first light, then turning to rose and finally white as the African sun climbed straight up into the sky. Near Amboseli we found elephant, buffalo, Masai giraffe, impala and gazelles. We saw three adult rhinos. One of them was earless, almost tail-less and with lots of red sores which were being actively explored by several oxpeckers. This could only be Pixie – the son of the very famous Gertie with her thirty-nine-inch-long horn who was killed by poachers. We did not see many lions but one pair had small cubs and we left them well alone. Bat-eared foxes were a new species for us and quite a few could be seen sitting around the entrances to their burrows, looking like small grey jackals with enormous ears. One special delight was the sight of four cheetahs – which are now so rare in Africa – squatting in the shade of a yellow-barked acacia and gazing longingly at a Thomson's gazelle feeding some distance away.

It was very pleasant to sit at Ol Tukai Lodge among the geraniums, petunias and ipomaeas and look across to the snowy cone of Kilimanjaro. As the day wore on, the summit was usually wreathed and then finally engulfed by cloud. From time to time a yellow 'dust-devil' would suddenly begin to spin round and track rapidly across the parched grassland. A lilac-breasted roller sat on top of a pole – a study in bronze and ultramarine. The uncommon and very beautiful Taveta golden weavers came to feed at the tables, sometimes in the company of glossy starlings, while fire finches crept about among the chairs like 'animated plums'.

We visited the Masai village near Namanga, which lay inside a protective thorn hedge. The cattle are driven each night into the compound and their dung soon raises the floor level. As Thelma and I approached the entrance, a sharp smell of urine and defaecation and a thick cloud of grey flies assailed us. We made our tour over a soft quaking floor of cow dung. On the right-hand side of the gateway was the hut of the chief wife, built of interwoven branches and roofed with hides plastered with more dung. The chief collected our entrance fee. The chief wife, adorned with red, white and blue beads stitched on leather and with holes in her ears big enough to put your fist through, squatted on the compost heap. She was working on a bead necklace and on her lap was an eighteen-month-old baby with a nasal discharge whose face was so covered in flies that it was quite impossible to distinguish any of her features.

The wildlife of Africa is a priceless asset for the whole of mankind, but there are also men living there with their own needs and hopes. The problem of reconciling the demands of both is a difficult one. In September 1961 the Arusha Declaration underlined the value of Africa's animals not only as a source of wonder and inspiration but also as 'an integral part of our natural resources and of our future livelihood and wellbeing'. Thelma and I had been on a kind of pilgrimage to see the world when it was young. Once you have been to Africa you are never quite the same again.

17

Wildlife on the World Service

In the summer of 1967 I made the momentous decision to leave the staff of the BBC and become a freelance broadcaster and writer. Almost immediately a piece of great good fortune came my way. I was talking in the foyer of Broadcasting House to Jack Singleton, an old friend and colleague and the producer for many years of the *Home in the Afternoon* programme. I told him of my decision to become a freelance and he said, 'Why don't you give Michael Pickstock a ring in Bush House? He's just about to start a new natural history and conservation series on the World Service of the BBC.' This I promptly did and Michael and I met the next day to discuss the programmes. At the end of our talk he invited me to become the presenter of this new weekly series. By 1975 the programme, known as *Nature Notebook*, had logged well over 400 editions, each broadcast three or four times a week over eight years.

Michael Pickstock had joined the BBC's World Service in 1964 to produce a weekly agricultural programme, but he began to feel, as he said, 'that an important element was missing from World Service output'. As an agriculturalist he had worked in Canada and New Zealand and travelled in Australia and Sri Lanka, where he had seen farming systems operating close to bush and forests full of wildlife. In his *Farming World* programme, with its concentration on techniques and productivity, there was little room for items on wildlife. So he made the first suggestion for a weekly programme in early 1966, but it was turned down on the grounds that natural history was really only of interest to Europeans and Americans and not to the bulk of World Service listeners in the tropics. The suggestion was again put forward in the spring of 1967 and this time received the blessing of Douglas Muggeridge who was then Head of Overseas Talks and Features.

Basically *Nature Notebook* has tried to reflect the situation of the world's wildlife over the years – its fascinating variety, the life systems and styles of different plant and animal species, the threats and pressures, and the attempts being made to conserve both the threatened species and their habitats. To have been associated with such a programme over eight years has been both a privilege and a responsibility and to have contributed to a better understanding and concern for the world's living things has been eminently satisfying. We have, in fact, reflected the wildlife of a hundred different countries in the world from Svalbard to the South Pole itself, and from places as remote as Campbell Island, Patagonia and Greenland. Many of the major conservation items have come, as one might expect, from Africa, India and Pakistan.

In Zambia, John Hanks gave an account of the breeding behaviour of elephants and the vexed question of culling them, and we were able to compare his experiences with those of Iain Douglas-Hamilton at Lake Manyara in East Africa. We included interviews with Joy Adamson who was studying cheetahs, with Jane van Lawick Goodall who was researching into the family life of chimpanzees and with Hans Kruuk who changed the image of the spotted hyaena. Dr Robert Martin reported for us on the state of the lemurs of Madagascar.

From India our contributors have included Zafar Futehally – a Vice-President of IUCN – who pointed out that there is always a conflict between the pure conservationist who hates the sight of other human beings like himself in a natural environment and others with a more developed fellow feeling who want the beauty and variety of nature to be enjoyed by as many people as possible. Balakrishna Seshadri – author of *The Twilight of India's Wildlife* – and Hari Dang of the Wildlife Preservation Society of India painted a rather gloomy picture for us. We have also had detailed accounts on the lions of Gir from Paul Joslin, on the tigers from Richard Waller of the World Wildlife Fund and on the Indian rhinos of Kaziranga from P. D. Stracey. I also interviewed Philip Wayre, who has taken part in many editions of the programme, after his official invitation to visit Bhutan which was not open to visitors; he gave us a vivid picture of the golden langur monkeys that he saw there. I also talked to Dr Duncan Poore, the Director of the Nature Conservancy, and Guy Mountfort who took part in exploratory investigations into the wildlife of Pakistan where spotted cats, snakes, lizards, birds of prey and many wild sheep, deer, goats and antelopes were in danger from hunting and the destruction of their natural environment. Many reports have come to us from south-east Asia, where our contributors have included Professor T. H. Harrisson on the orang-outang, Nigel Sitwell on Bawean deer, Lord Medway on cave swiftlets and Michael Tweedie who provided us with portraits of turtles, water buffaloes and the rare bird-wing butterflies, one of which was auctioned in Paris in 1967 for as much as 2500 dollars.

Australia, with its unique marsupial fauna, has often been featured in our programme, with accounts ranging from the biology of kangaroos, by the world's authority Professor Geoffrey Sharman, to investigations into echidnas, giant seven-foot-long earthworms, coral reefs and the Crown of Thorns starfish, and Australasian fleas. In the same way New Zealand has supplied us with stories about the biology of kiwis, the strange living fossil – the tuatara – the takahe, the kakapo, and the rediscovery of the North Island thrush.

North America is very conservation-minded and we have received a number of letters from Canada and the United States. We have featured great conservation matters like the draining and burning of the Everglades, the effects of DDT on pelicans, whale and seal hunting, the oil industry in Alaska, and we have looked in detail at animals from the great wood bison down to the devil's hole pupfish with the most restricted range of any vertebrate – a single spring hole in Nevada. Nor have we neglected South and Central America, with reports on Guyana and Trinidad from Dr David Snow, who is the head of the Bird Room of the British Museum of Natural History, and Janet Coates Barber of the World Wildlife Fund whom I interviewed about the plants and animals of Costa Rica, Panama and El Salvador. Perhaps one of the most colourful visitors to Bush House whom I talked to was Dr Felipé Benavides, the

President of the National Parks of Peru and former Consul-General in London. He had come to try and save the vicuña – a wild llama, once sacred to the Incas, whose numbers had fallen from 200 000 at the turn of the century to between 8000 and 10 000 in 1968. A trade in vicuña skins was still going on in Britain, although the killing of the animals in Peru was illegal. Recently the numbers have improved and in 1973 there had been a 160 per cent increase from the 1968 total. Roger Perry, who is the son of the horticulturalist Frances Perry, and was my sound recording successor in the BBC in 1958, became Director of the Charles Darwin Research Station on the Galapagos Islands, from which he gave us vivid reports on the finches and giant tortoises of these 'enchanted islands'. He also explored Colombia, where, according to the latest count, there are more species of bird – 1556 – than in any other country in the world.

By using experts in their field we have tried to show something of the variety that exists in the world of Nature and also the way in which scientists approach it from the point of view of research and possible techniques of conservation. Our news items have been very varied and we have reported both the welcome and the less welcome with equal impartiality to forestall the critics who say that conservationists are always prophets of doom.

From time to time various expeditions have set out to investigate little-known parts of the earth and many of these have been represented in *Nature Notebook*. Lieutenant-Colonel John Blashford-Snell, who led the British Trans-America Expedition, recalled his experiences crossing the humid and difficult Darien Gap – 'a land of snakes, insects and friendly Indians' where Panama meets South America. We broadcast Derek Bromhall's account of his journey through the cloud forests on the table mountain of Roraima – Conan Doyle's 'Lost World'. Ian Bishop led the 1967–9 Royal Society Expedition to the Mato Grosso and talked to us about the wildlife of the region. Dr Adam Locket described his expedition to the Comoro Islands to examine a live coelacanth and we heard about Dr Adrian Marshall's trip to the New Hebrides.

Nearer home I also introduced the idea of a 'walkabout'

edition of *Nature Notebook*, derived from my domestic radio *Countryside* programmes. I visited a certain region of wildlife interest in Britain and talked to a local naturalist on the spot about the area, its geography and history, wildlife and problems of conservation. I toured Minsmere with Herbert Axell, where we talked about migration, and Jeremy Sorensen showed me the Ouse Washes. Ted Ellis rowed me round Wheatfen Broad, where the coypus had their home, and Douglas Willis shared with me the whooper swans and other wild-fowl treasures of Aberdeenshire's Loch of Strathbeg. I watched my first waxwings – birds which had eluded me all my life – at Leighton Moss with John Wilson in December 1974, and I visited the ospreys of Speyside with Ian Hopkins.

Conservation has figured continuously in our programmes and we have reported the work and aims of the International Union for Conservation of Nature and Natural Resources. The World Wildlife Fund has helped us keep up to date and we have broadcast interviews with Dr Luc Hoffmann, a Vice-President, as well as Dr Fritz Vollmar, the Director-General, Dr Hartmut Jungius, and Trustee Guy Mountfort. In a discussion for *Nature Notebook* that I had with Sir Peter Scott, Vice-President and Chairman of the World Wildlife Fund, he described how the money for the British Appeal might come from single gifts as large as £100 000 to pennies placed in wishing wells and collecting boxes. The money was used to buy or rent land, purchase equipment, pay wardens and assist research.

As will become clear in the next chapter, I became responsible for producing a series of wildlife records for BBC Radio Enterprises later called BBC Records; these were based on the BBC's Sound Archives and included many of the recordings that I had made. One of these records on which I worked for over a year was a conservation disk entitled *Wildlife in Danger*. It was derived directly from our *Nature Notebook* programmes. On the front side were spoken contributions from ten of the world's leading conservationists, seven of which had already been broadcast in our series on the World Service. It was introduced by the President of IUCN, Harold J. Coolidge, and included other contributions from Noel Simon, Colonel Jack

Vincent, Professor T. H. Harrisson, Dr Ernst Lang, Sir Peter Scott, Philip Wayre, Dr R. D. Martin and Dr L. Harrison Matthews. The second side of the record carried the sounds of fifty-nine animals whose full species or geographical races were in danger of extinction. Among them was the squeak of the aye aye from Madagascar, of which not more than about fifty live in the wild, and the trumpet of the Japanese crested ibis whose numbers were down to about ten. From Western Australia came a recording of the noisy scrub bird once thought to have disappeared for ever but which was rediscovered in November 1961 at Two People Bay east of Albany. There are now perhaps between fifty and a hundred birds. Prince Philip showed a great personal interest in the colony, which is now fully protected.

I thought it would be a pleasant gesture to send Prince Philip a copy of the record *Wildlife in Danger* and this he very graciously accepted. In his personal letter to me he expressed the belief that the conservation of nature needed to be explained over and over again to a predominantly urban population. We have tried to do this in *Nature Notebook*. It was Mrs Gandhi, Prime Minister of India, who said that 'modern man must re-establish an unbroken link with nature and with life'.

18

Broadcasting House

In 1943, when Thelma and I were based at the RAF Station at Barford St John, we went into the Officers' Mess late one evening after a visit to Oxford to try to persuade the WAAF waitress to organize some sandwiches for us. She was a cheerful pleasant girl who specialized in telling fortunes and she had been trying to waylay me for some time. That night she insisted on reading the tea leaves in my cup and with some amusement I agreed. Among her prognostications was one that said that I would spend a large part of my life in a large functional concrete and stone building – at the time a rather forbidding prospect. Years later I realized that she had painted a very convincing picture of Broadcasting House in London!

In my early days in what we all called 'B.H.' I spent many hours building up the wildlife section of the BBC's Sound Archives, selecting and then processing into disks not only the recordings that I had obtained myself but also material from sources outside the BBC. These included recordings by Sture Palmér made for Sweden's Sveriges Radio, by Carl Weismann in Denmark, by the Victor Recording Company of Japan and by the University of Western Australia. Horizon Pictures, who made the film *The Bridge on the River Kwai*, sent me their recordings of flying foxes, amphibians and jungle atmospheres made in Ceylon. Dr W. J. L. (Bill) Sladen visited Signy Island in the South Orkneys in 1951 with a wire recorder and brought back the first recordings of Adelie and chinstrap penguins and Antarctic skuas. Bill told me that the wire from his recorder was marvellous for sutures! Dr Michael Swales also made some fine recordings of petrels, shearwaters, the wandering albatross and the Gough Island bunting from that remote island in the South Atlantic. Nearer home an amateur, John Kirby, was making bird recordings on the Yorkshire moors with a home-made tape recorder based on a portable clockwork gramophone and he was to become a regular contributor to the Sound Archives.

I was gradually building up a fairly representative collection of the sounds of British and West European birds. I also worked towards an agreement with Cornell University in the United States to exchange natural history material on an equal basis. It was a matter for regret that I left to go to television before I could see that the arrangement with Cornell was brought fully to fruition. From 1958 Roger Perry, who was appointed to the new post of Librarian and Field Research Assistant in the new Natural History Unit at Bristol, extended the collection from his own expeditions and from a growing external flow of sound recordings as battery-operated tape recorders became more available. In May 1962 he resigned and wrote to me to say that he had found it 'a most pleasant and rewarding experience following along in this field'. He was succeeded by John F. Burton, who was a former assistant secretary at the British Trust for Ornithology. He turned his attention very much towards acquiring good atmosphere recordings of various habitats and towards the selection of material from outside contributors. After I had left the BBC John invited me to help him with that latter task especially as by 1968 no fewer than 110 individuals and bodies had offered wildlife recordings to the Corporation.

I have also continued to make my own sound recordings and in the last few years I have been especially pleased to obtain those of great and Arctic skuas on the Fair Isle, of common scoters with their plaintive bell-like calls in County Fermanagh, of rutting fallow and Sika deer in the glades of the New Forest, of waxwings at Leighton Moss in Lancashire and of firecrests singing in a Buckinghamshire spruce wood. It took me more than twenty years to capture on tape the alarm notes of the hedgesparrow! When I was on Fair Isle in 1963 I recorded one of the island wrens singing near the Observatory, actually the first recording of this sub-species. Eleven years later I met Patrick Sellar at the Fifth Anniversary Celebration of the

Birds of the Air

British Library of Wildlife Sounds in South Kensington. He told me that his recording of a male wren holding territory in 1974 near the Observatory, analysed on sound spectrograms made by Joan Hall-Craggs, showed similiar patterns and range to mine and revealed a striking permanency over the years.

In January 1966 the BBC entered a new field. BBC Radio Enterprises, now BBC Records, was set up to exploit broadcast material – both from radio and television – in the form of long-playing gramophone records for sale to the public both at home and abroad. The first production was *Sir Malcolm Sargent – Music Maker*. This proved to be a best seller and it was soon followed by others based on broadcasts by Freddie Grisewood and Sir John Betjeman.

Easter 1969 saw the launching of a new series of Wildlife Records. The first, *A Salute to Ludwig Koch*, was produced by John F. Burton in Bristol and included a commentary by Desmond Hawkins and many of Ludwig's bird recordings. John Burton was kind enough to suggest to Jack Aistrop that I produce for BBC Records something that was very close to my heart – an identification disk of British mammal and amphibian sounds. It appeared in September 1969 and carried recordings of thirty-eight mammals on the British list and six amphibians. As far as I know, this was the first mammal record guide issued in Europe.

This was the beginning of an interesting and pleasant period of work and during the next three years I produced no fewer than fourteen LP disks in the *Wildlife* and other series. *Sounds of the Countryside*, which proved a very successful record, provided a seasonal picture of British wildlife and was based on my *Countryside* radio programmes, while *Woodland Birds*, which was issued at the same time as my New Naturalist volume of the same name, provided a guide to bird songs from January to December. I dedicated *Sea and Island Birds* to a lasting friend and great ornithologist – James Fisher – who died so tragically in an accident in 1970 not far from my home. We also issued a bird identification record to accompany the television series *A Year's Journey* which I was presenting and which was being viewed by more than 15 000 classes in 9000 schools. In 1973 at the invitation of the National Trust, I prepared a special record of the sounds of nature, many of which I had obtained on Trust properties over the years.

There was one other disk which did not fall into the previous groups and which was also a great pleasure to produce. I spent two days with Sir Peter Scott, whom I had interviewed a number of times before, and recorded a discussion at his home in Slimbridge. He talked freely to me about his life from his early schoolboy days to his latest expeditions. This was a very personal record of a man's life and development.

Just across the road from Broadcasting House, opposite the Langham Hotel where BBC Records have their headquarters, is the brick-built block of No. 1 Portland Place. This is the base of BBC School Broadcasting (Radio). Its present head is Charles Armour – a friendly and dedicated educationalist to whom I owe a great deal as a broadcaster. In a single year there are more than eighty radio series and nearly forty television series, while the BBC's twenty local radio stations, guided by Educational Panels in which the School Broadcasting Council has vested its responsibilities, broadcast some 4000 educational programmes every year. Many programmes are also taped for future use and radiovision, with its blending of a colour film-strip and a radio broadcast, has brought a new experience and teaching aid to the schools. Today some 33 000 schools use radio. While 90 per cent of all schools in the United Kingdom take advantage of radio broadcasts about 80 per cent follow television transmissions. But I am sure that the full potential of the service offered has not yet been realized. Dame Margaret Miles, whose views on education I respect, said that 'Radio and television have been best used in the schools where teachers have made full use of the excellent supporting material available, and ancillary activities like tape-recording programmes.' Those of us who have visited schools would agree with this, I am sure.

I first broadcast for Schools Radio way back in 1955 and I continued an unbroken association into the era of the *Nature* series that replaced it. After I had become a freelance in 1967 I was asked to become a consultant to Margaret (Meg) Sheffield – a New Zealander who had come to England in 1965, and was producing the *Nature* programmes. Besides acting as a consultant, I also wrote scripts and presented programmes on such varied topics as eels, clouded yellow butterflies, the simple ecology of woodlands, and the dawn chorus.

In 1969 Meg Sheffield was asked by the School Broadcasting Council to prepare two radiovision film strips on sex education for primary schools within the framework of the *Nature* series – a new departure for the BBC. Both of my children read the scripts at an early stage. David, who was nine at the time, approved it, finding in it nothing that he did not already know or that was difficult to understand. Amanda, who was seven and a half, said, 'There's something that I don't understand, Daddy!'

'Yes?' I replied, thinking that one of the words or terms was new to her, or perhaps too technical.

'It's that!' she said, pointing at the script with a finger.

'Oh! That!' I exclaimed, as I peered over her shoulder. 'That's a semi-colon!'

When Peter Ward took over the *Nature* series not long afterwards I continued with the consultancy work, taking part in planning meetings, discussing programmes and their presenters, checking scripts and helping with the publications – all work that I very much enjoy. I was also asked to present programmes and went off to gather interviews and sounds. This might involve tours of rubbish dumps in a search for town foxes, crawling through blackbird roosts or watching bird migration on the east coast. I travelled up to Scotland and recorded two programmes with Dick Balharry in Wester Ross where we tramped over grouse moors, stalked red deer and rowed out to the islands on Loch Maree. The highlight was a two-way radio conversation which I recorded as Dick climbed up a difficult face to a golden eagle's eyrie.

Recently I completed a radiovision filmstrip for my young schools radio listeners on how to take up bird-watching – an audience anxious and willing to learn. In 1975 Peter Ward and I worked on a programme about the natural history of Buckingham Palace. We were the first to be granted permission for a radio programme of this kind and Prince Philip agreed to be interviewed by me. During a six-hour watch in the palace garden in May 1975, I observed 216 wild birds of no fewer than twenty-five species.

I have also taken part in educational programmes for a much older age group than primary schools. In 1974 I presented a feature on whale-hunting for the Middle Years, while six years earlier Rosemary Jellis of BBC Further Education approached me to find out whether I would be willing to act as a presenter for three programmes in 'Study on Three' for an adult audience. The series was to be called *Bird Sounds and their Meanings*. Having spent so many years in collecting and investigating bird songs and calls I was delighted to accept. The first programme was devoted to song, the second to the range of a bird's language and the third to the techniques of sound recordings. We invited Kenneth Williamson, Dr J. M. Cullen, John Borwick, Patrick Sellar and the late Terry Gompertz to take part. The series was repeated in the summer of 1969 with an additional programme on birds as musicians. It included a contribution from Joan Hall-Craggs, well known for her study and recordings of blackbird songs. This programme was entered for the 1970 Japan Prize.

Broadcasting House has seen me pacing its corridors, working in its recording channels and broadcasting from its studios for a quarter of a century. To it over the years have come many letters and parcels addressed to me. Some of the letters like those from Freddie Grisewood, Basil Radford, Peter Cushing and others have been chatty 'birdy' or other communications about animals while others have asked for information. And then there was the dead bird which arrived in a sweet-smelling lavender box from a listener who wrote to me: 'I can't find a picture of this bird in my bird book. *Nature Parliament* keep saying in their programme, "Don't please send us any specimens to identify!" But I thought of you and rather than put it in the dustbin I'm posting it off to you. I hope you don't mind!' Nor did I mind! This bird, which had been found dead in Furness Road in Eastbourne, was only the eighteenth yellow-billed cuckoo from America ever to be recorded in the British Isles.

I included some of these stories in a special programme, marking the fiftieth anniversary of the BBC, which was broadcast in 1972 and was produced by Dilys Breese. It was a natural history tour of Broadcasting House which I provided for the programme's presenter, Derek Jones. To quote the *Radio Times*: 'Today's Radio Nature Trail celebrates the BBC's fiftieth anniversary with a bird-watching trip round our own man-made environment, Broadcasting House, in London'. We talked about the breeding feral pigeons, the scavenging sparrows and gulls, the starling flyways that passed overhead from Dollis Hill and north-west London to Trafalgar Square, the black redstarts that used to sing from the masts and the migrating chaffinches, pipits and wagtails that I watched from the roof of B.H. in the 1950s.

As Derek Jones and I stood on the roof of Broadcasting House, I told him about the kestrels that used to nest in a ventilator hole in the ornate façade of the BBC's Langham Hotel across the road, and which Geoffrey Mulligan and I had filmed nearly a decade earlier. The ventilator was unfortunately bricked up during the cleaning operations for the fiftieth anniversary celebrations. Despite powerful efforts by John Crawley, the Assistant to the Director-General, to get a kestrel box which was supplied by Dilys Breese, fitted to the front of the Langham at a point which I suggested, the cost and the problems raised by the Town and Country Planning Act proved insurmountable.

As part of these same fiftieth anniversary celebrations Thelma and I were invited to a Television Service reception in the Television Centre at the White City. The other guests included George Cansdale, Harry Carpenter, Dandy Nicholls, Frank Windsor, Geoffrey Keene, Barbara Kelly and Bernard Braden. It was pleasant to talk to Joyce Grenfell, who is herself a very keen bird-watcher. It was an intimate and very enjoyable occasion and contrasted very much in my mind with the thirtieth anniversary celebrations which I attended when the BBC took the Empress Hall at Earls Court for two consecutive nights.

19
Backwards and Forwards

I am writing this final chapter in my garden room at Dollis Hill. A blue tit is hanging upside down from a pink plastic net full of peanuts a foot from the window. A few feet away a hen blackbird is looking for worms on the lawn. I can see a trickle of migrant redwings and a magpie passing overhead. My yellow Labrador Argus is lying asleep at my feet. I can think of no better situation than this for me to contemplate what has been a full, creative and very active life – slowed now just a little by past surgery. It has been a life spent in close contact with living things and thus the fulfilment of many youthful hopes and ambitions.

Of course, a great deal of my present effort, as one who joined what C. Gordon Glover called 'the thrombostic ranks of the freelance writers and broadcasters', has been directed towards radio and television. The *A Year's Journey* series has been running for three years, with its last twenty-eight programmes in colour. Felicia Elwell and I have journeyed with a camera unit all over the British Isles and have visited Eire, Holland and France. Our travels took us to such varied locations as the slate quarries at Blaenau Ffestiniog, the bird island of Rathlin seven miles off the coast of Antrim, the megalithic 'alignments' at Carnac and the broken sixty-foot-long standing stone at Locmariaquer. While I was in France I traced the history of William the Conqueror from his birthplace at Falaise to Bayeux, where we were privileged to film the Tapestry, to Mont St Michel, and to Caen, which I had not seen since the raid of 1944 and which had been completely rebuilt. From filmed portraits of King's Lynn and Liverpool we flew to Holland to see how the Dutch had won their land from the sea. We filmed down a salt mine in Cheshire and in the Potteries. We travelled to Galway to shoot sequences on the limestone Burren and we sailed across to the Isle of Inishmore in the Aran Islands.

The most stimulating part of a freelance's life is that he can never be quite sure when he may be invited to take part in or prepare a programme over and above those for which he has long term contracts. I have very much enjoyed participating in *The Living World* natural history programmes from Bristol, sometimes as a contributor on a special subject or as an invited member of the *Talking Point* team, which tries to answer listeners' questions, when I have joined such well-known figures as Dr Maurice Burton, Dr Ernest Neal, Phil Drabble and Ted Ellis. Since I live only five miles or so from Broadcasting House in London, Bush House, the Television Centre, Lime Grove and the Ealing Film Studios I can respond easily to sudden phone calls. These may invite me to answer questions or give opinions on the television programme *Nationwide*. Bob Wellings has interviewed me about an unusually early spring and Sue Lawley on London foxes and how the drought in the Sahel in Africa was affecting our migrant birds. Once I had the pleasant experience of sharing the make-up room with both Lynsey De Paul and the Foreign Secretary, Mr James Callaghan, and on another occasion I met old Latymerian Mr Peter Walker. I have taken part in such radio series as *Today*, *The World at One*, *P.M.*, and *You and Yours*. As an interviewer myself I quite enjoy having the roles reversed and finding myself quizzed by William Hardcastle about suburban birds, by Sue MacGregor on the first cuckoo in spring and Nigel Murphy on the cult of bird-watching.

Woman's Hour and *Motoring and the Motorist* have asked for contributions on topical matters of natural history, such as culling seals or the slaughter of wildlife on the road. And in Bush House I have provided talks for the current affairs programme *Outlook* on many subjects and contributed to features on introduced animals, animal display and the Ice Age, as well as answering such questions as 'Do hens enjoy sex?' on *Postmark Africa*. In 1974 I took part in half a dozen programmes in the British Forces Broadcasting Service series

Man Around which were presented by Douglas Cameron, formerly of the BBC *Today* programme. Then in 1975 I presented twelve monthly programmes on wildlife for BBC Local Radio. These were produced by Hal Bethell and were taken by thirteen of the twenty local radio stations.

In the summer of 1973 John Burton of the Natural History Unit in Bristol invited me to join a recording expedition to the Camargue to obtain stereo recordings of the wildlife – the first expedition of this kind abroad – and to present a feature in stereo for Radio 4. With sound recordists David Tombs and Brian Martin we navigated a twenty-five-foot cabin cruiser from Palavas-les-Flots on the Mediterranean to St Gilles on the edge of the Camargue by following the course of the Canal du Rhône. For me this was a return after an absence of nineteen years and John wanted me to describe my reaction to the changes that had taken place since 1954. Once again I gazed at a colony of breeding flamingoes – perhaps 4000 birds – at the gorgeous bee-eaters excavating their holes by the roadside at Petit Badon and at the black-winged stilts yelping over their soggy marshes. And there were changes. The roads were wider and faster, aircraft flew over to get a low bird's-eye view of the nesting flamingoes, many of the waterways were heavily polluted and the skyline was now dominated by chimneys belching smoke and flame.

We collected the first stereo recordings of some twenty-five different species of bird, together with those of tree frogs, crickets and typical atmospheres in different habitats in the Camargue. All my narration for the radio programme was given on the spot and recorded in stereo with the natural sounds going on behind or even all round me. The finished programme, called *A Return to the Camargue*, was broadcast in September 1973 as part of a special week of stereo programmes mounted by the BBC.

I have spent a considerable amount of time in recent years trying to give warning of the dangers that threaten our natural world and its wildlife in the belief that awareness is the first step to concern and then perhaps to action. Through the medium of external broadcasting it has been possible to do this on a global scale, but I am sure that we can do a lot in our own communities. The London Borough of Brent, where I live, is becoming more and more receptive to conservation ideas as they are offered them. The borough has established a nature reserve near the Welsh Harp for use by local schoolchildren on land that might easily have been developed. When I gave a sermon on 'Harvest and the Endangered Earth' in St Catherine's parish church at Neasden, the mayor, a number of the councillors and a local member of parliament attended. This service was shared between the vicar, the Reverend David Barlow (now Chaplain at Cranleigh School), and myself, and I used sound recordings and colour slides to show how we were misusing the world's resources and degrading the environment in which we lived. At my suggestion the local authority cleared some disused allotments for a new school before the breeding season to avoid slaughtering many eggs and young birds. I was also able to dissuade London Transport from cutting the grass in summer on some of their rail embankments where several species of the less common butterflies had colonies.

In October 1972 a Conservation Group was set up to try to protect our local reservoir – the Welsh Harp – from industrial and residential development. I am a founder member of the group and the chairman, Leo Batten, has written very lucidly about the birdlife in *Birdwatchers' Year*. The group was represented at a three-day public enquiry early in 1974 where, with Brent and Barnet Councils, it opposed the development of open-space land near the water for blocks of expensive flats. Half the time was occupied by the group's evidence – an indication of what a voluntary local group can do, and we won a limited victory. I also entered the lists on behalf of another piece of water close to my heart – the Loch of Strathbeg in Aberdeenshire – the largest coastal dune lake in the British Isles. This large, unpolluted loch can hold up to ten species of breeding duck and in winter 9000 grey lag and pink-footed geese, several thousand pochard, wigeon and tufted duck, 500 goldeneye and 800 whooper swans. It was threatened by the proposed North Sea pipelines of the British Gas Corporation and Total Oil Marine which would have passed through the dunes and loch. No one could be against developments that would bring employment, economic growth and new reserves of fuel and power to Scotland, but Buchan was facing growing industrialization and there ought to be compromises between the new growth and the landscape. The strength of local conservationists finally persuaded the Gas Corporation and Total Oil to site their terminal to the south at St Fergus. There is a disused airfield near the Loch that could be used for several purposes and there is still need for vigilance. Richard Baker, the BBC television news reader, tells me that he was stationed on this airfield for a short time during the last war.

In 1972 I was appointed to the Committee on Bird Sanctuaries in the Royal Parks. Its chairman was Lord Hurcomb, whom I had known for many years and who had held the chairmanship since the committee was set up in April 1947 by the then Minister of Works. Lord Hurcomb retired in 1974 and his place was taken by Stanley Cramp, for many years Chairman of the RSPB Council. The purpose of the committee was to advise the Department of the Environment which had the statutory responsibility for seeing that the Parks are properly cared for. At our meetings we have discussed many recommendations to improve the value of the Royal Parks both as open spaces for recreation and as areas attractive to birds. The committee is helped by official observers and by periodical reports on the birdlife. In 1974 Her Majesty's Stationery Office published my *Wild Life in the Royal Parks* which I had written at the invitation of the Department of the Environment. Shortly before its publication the Right Honourable Geoffrey Rippon, who was then Secretary of State for the Environment, gave a reception in his rooms in Admiralty House in honour of the observers and the members of the committee.

Aristotle said that you must wait until the evening before you can tell what sort of day it has been. I suppose that for me it might be said that on this time scale I have just finished my five o'clock tea! Even from that viewpoint I am quite sure that I can look back on a very happy and rewarding life. I recognize that there were distinct advantages from the start – devoted and Christian parents who made great sacrifices so that, like my brothers and sister, I could reach university. As the youngest child I benefited from my parents' growing experience of parenthood, an improved standard of living and the encouragement, wisdom and stimulation of my siblings. I met many people of varied backgrounds and interests, and my schooldays, despite several bouts of ill-health, were pleasant and full of activity. My life was spared during the war and I suffered no injury or disablement. Because of it I met my wife. I am pleased that my early association with education has gone on and I have embraced the cause of conservation, very seriously concerned, but with some degree of hope, for I am basically an optimist. I have visited some of the most magnificent places on the earth and I have met a very large number of people many of whom should be, although few are, represented in this book. I value the friendships which I have made and I am grateful for the associations which have rewarded my professional life.

I thank my Maker that I have the use of my senses – my ears to hear the songs and calls of birds, the hum of insects, Shakespeare declaimed well, the voices of loved ones and the music of Beethoven, and my sense of smell to delight me when I contemplate an old-fashioned rose and walk in an oakwood after rain. My eyes have given me an inexhaustible reservoir of images – a kingfisher in flight, bluebells in spring, the smile of a baby, dawn on Kilimanjaro, the Parthenon in the golden light of evening, Manhattan, the face of an old friend – there is so much for me to draw upon. Over the years, as I have mellowed, I have tried to learn the value of tolerance and what I hope are my now less-frequent bouts of petulance were, I fear, brought about by an impatience to do things my way. I have not spared myself physically or mentally, for how can one go slow on something so satisfying?

Some people may think that the study of birds is a rather trivial pursuit and ask what relevance or value there can be in giving time and effort to them. Particularly might this criticism be levelled at me when we are in the throes of an economic crisis. My answer is that within small limits I have helped to advance man's knowledge of those other creatures with whom he shares the earth. Fresh knowledge cannot surely in itself be bad. And I would also add that if we do not care about birds and other animals we may not care how we treat each other. They all evolved long before man in an environment which itself enabled man to grow and flourish.

Backwards and Forwards

I look forward to seeing my children grow up. I hope that that they will find real happiness and a quality of life that we have not totally degraded for them. If they can wish to care about other people and show concern for them this alone makes life worth living. If I look ahead I cannot be sure of the future but man has proved surprisingly adaptable in the past. It will not be easy for them.

I still hope to do many things. I trust that there are more sound recordings to make, more broadcasts to give, more research to undertake, more books to write – and I am currently working on another New Naturalist book for Collins. All these things may not now take place far from home but closer to my native air, where, like Alexander Pope, I shall hope to spend the evening of my day and find the hours slip away.

> In health of body, peace of mind,
> Quiet by day,
> Sound sleep by night; study and ease
> Together mixed.

Chronology

1921	Born
1927	Started school
1932	Latymer Upper School (to 1939)
1937	London Natural History Society
1939	Merton College. Oxford Ornithological Society. University Air Squadron
1941	RAF (to 1946)
1942–43	United States. Canada. Westmorland. Commissioned
1943	Married. Operations over Europe. Battle of Berlin
1944	Battle of France. Awarded D.F.C. Join staff of Bomber Command Instructors' School. Crew N.C.O.'s commissioned
1945	Honeymoon in Cornwall
1946	Demobbed. M.A. Diploma in Education at Oxford
1947	Schoolmaster in Rugby. West Midland Bird Club. Holland
1948–50	Teaching in Stratford-upon-Avon. Cotswold migration route. Scotland. Lecturing for Birmingham University
1950	Elected to British Ornithologists' Union. First radio broadcast. Appointed to BBC
1951	Evesham. Broadcasting House, London. Introduce tape and parabolic reflectors to wildlife recording. Badgers. 'Rocket-netting' geese. London Zoo. Dollis Hill
1952	*Bird Migrants* published. Start *Countryside of the Month* radio programme. Hilbre. Minsmere. 'Midget' portable tape recorders
1953	Elected to Council of Royal Society for the Protection of Birds and a Fellow of Zoological Society. Breckland. Scottish Highlands
1954	Camargue and Provence. Address XIth International Ornithological Congress at Basel. Join British Ornithologists Club and British Trust for Ornithology. Norfolk.

Chronology

1955	Slimbridge. First use of radio links for wildlife recording. *The Songs and Calls of British Birds* published. Farne Islands. Norfolk. Scotland. First hydrophone recordings of fish.
1956	France. Spain. British Transport Films
1957	*Voices of the Wild* published. Appointed to Laboratory of Ornithology at Cornell University. Scottish Highlands. Minsmere
1958	Father died. *Witherby's Sound Guide to British Birds* published. Join BBC Television. Filming on Skomer Island and at Field Study Centres. *Birds* television series with James Fisher
1959	Television series *Mammals in Britain* and *The Insect World*. Filming in the Highlands, Norfolk and Devon. France and Switzerland. Migration watches in Alps
1960	David born. Television series *Birds in Winter*. Filming in Breckland, Sussex, Kent, Northumberland and on Farne Islands
1961	Amanda born. Filming at Great Tew (until 1962) for series of twenty-eight *A Year in the Country* programmes. Voyage to remote Scottish islands
1962	Mother died. *A Study of Suburban Bird-Life at Dollis Hill* published
1963	*The BBC Book of the Countryside* published. Filming on Fair Isle, in Scottish Highlands, New Forest, East Anglia
1964	Filming wildlife at Minsmere and in New Forest
1965	Appointed Justice of the Peace. Television series *Frontiers for Man*. The Countryside in 1970 Conference. Begin filming *A Year's Journey* in Shetland and northern Scotland. Hebrides and the Isles of Scilly. Safari to Uganda, Kenya and Tanzania
1966	Filming in Wales, Outer Hebrides, Caithness and Sutherland
1967	Sabbatical leave. Visit Scotland, Ulster and Eire. Resign from BBC. *Nature Notebook* starts on BBC World Service. Consultant to BBC Schools Radio
1968	Silver wedding. Remake *A Year's Journey*. Lake District. Isles of Scilly. South-west Ireland
1969	*Witherby's Sound Guide to British Birds* LP version published. Start work on fourteen LP wildlife discs for BBC Records. Begin shooting twenty-eight new colour films for *A Year's Journey*. Snowdonia. Isle of Wight. Ulster
1970	Filming in Ulster and on Rathlin Island. The Borders.

	Normandy and Brittany. Switzerland. Italy
1971	*Woodland Birds* published. Filming in Fenland, Holland, Cheshire, Galway and on Aran Islands. Italy, Switzerland and Liechtenstein
1972	Appointed to Committee on Bird Sanctuaries in the Royal Parks. Fiftieth anniversary radio programme about Broadcasting House. Hindson Memorial Lecture. Ouse Washes. Minsmere. Switzerland. Welsh Harp Conservation Group
1973	Stereo expedition with BBC Natural History Unit to Languedoc and Camargue. *Metroland* programme. Norfolk Broads. Kinross. Greece. Provence in autumn. Produce National Trust wildlife record
1974	*Wild Life in the Royal Parks* published. 500th television appearance and 3500th radio broadcast. British Forces Network series. Italy. Scotland. North Wales. Solway Firth
1975	*Birds of Town and Suburb* published. 250th *Countryside* and 400th *Nature Notebook* programme. First BBC Local Radio wildlife series. Radiovision on bird-watching. Buckingham Palace programme prepared. *Live and Let Live* published. Amanda a Queen's Guide. Vice-President of Friends of Beast Youth Symphony Orchestra. Highlands. North Wales. Isle of Wight
1976	Radio series *Voices of the Wild*

Index

aard-vaark, 147
accentor, alpine, 143
Adam, Kenneth, 108, 109
Africa, 146–63, 165, 185
Aistrop, Jack, 172
Alanbrooke, F/M Lord, 93, 116, 121
albatross, wandering, 170
alligator, 42, 45, 48
Alps, 141–4, 146
André, Pierre, 146, 148
anhinga, 46, 148, 149
Appleby, 33, 38, 39, 55, 56, 81
Armour, Charles, 173
Attenborough, David, 111, 128, 135, 138
auk, little, 39
Axell, H. E., 103–4, 168
aye-aye, 169

badger, 94–5, 109, 184
Bagnall-Oakeley, R. P. (Dick), 93, 97, 125, 126–7, 128–9
Baker, E. A., 43–4, 47
Baker, Richard, 181
Balharry, Dick, 174
Bannister, Sir Roger, 130
Batten, Leo, 180
Battle, of Berlin, 65–75, 184; of Britain, 32–3; of France, 76–8, 184
BBC: educational programmes, 110, 124–30, 132, 138, 172–5, 177–8, 185; external broadcasting, 48, 60, 111, 164–9, 178, 179, 185; local radio, 153, 179, 186; radio, 11, 13–15, 26, 89, 90, 91–2, 103–4, 108; 109, 110, 111, 112, 124, 126, 141, 164, 168–9, 170–6, 178, 179, 184, 185, 186; television, 124–31, 132, 159, 176, 178
bee-eater: European, 115, 116, 121, 156, 174; carmine, 153
Benavides, Dr Felipé, 166–7
Bernard, Nicolette, 21

Betjeman, Sir John, 141, 172
Beven, Dr Geoffrey, 24
Beveridge, Lord, 29
Bird Migrants, 85, 184
Birds of Town and Suburb, 140, 186
Bird Sounds and Their Meanings, 175
bison, wood, 166
bittern, 96, 137; least, 45; little, 115
blackbird, 103, 174, 177; rusty, 40
Blashford-Snell, Lt-Col John, 167
Blunden, Edmund, 28, 33
boar, wild, 114, 121
Bond, Sgt R. (Bob), 58, 61, 68
Bonsall, Frank, 28, 29, 81
Boswall, Jeffery, 92, 113
Bottomley, A/M Sir Norman, 64, 80
Breckenridge, Flt-Lt W. (Bill), 73–4
Breese, Dilys, 141, 176
British Forces Broadcasting Service, 178–9, 186
British Library of Wildlife Sounds, 172
British Ornithologists' Club, 112, 184
British Trust for Ornithology, 106, 171, 184
Broughshane, Lord, 21
Brown, Philip, 113
Buckingham Palace, 174–5, 186
buffalo: African, 150, 151, 154, 156, 161, 162; water, 166
Bullough, Prof. W. S., 104, 125, 129
bunting: cirl, 24; Gough Island, 170; ortolan, 119; rock, 119; snow, 89 97, 103
Burton, Flt-Lt George, 79, 87, 140
Burton, Humphrey, 111–12
Burton, John. F., 171, 172, 179
Burton, Dr Maurice, 178
bushbuck, 161
bush-chat, rufous, 121
bustard, Kori, 156

Cairngorms, 98–101, 133, 136
Callaghan, James, 178

Index

Camargue, 13–15, 106, 114–16, 143, 179, 184, 186
Campbell, Dr Bruce, 88, 125, 129
Canada, 40, 50–1, 53–4, 164, 166
Cansdale, George, 104, 176
cats: Siamese, 110; wild, 104
chaffinch, 140, 176
chamois, 143
cheetah, 156, 157, 162
chiffchaff, 24, 103
chimpanzee, 128, 165
chough, alpine, 143
Churchill, Sir Winston, 64, 104
Clay, Theresa, 22
Clement, Keith, 126
Cley-next-the-Sea, 97–8, 103, 126
coelacanth, 167
Coles, Henry (Grandfather), 16, 27
Collenette, C. L., 24
Constantine, Lord, 144
Coolidge, Harold J., 168
coot, 115, 122; red-knobbed, 160
cormorant, 83; white-necked, 149
corncrake, 24, 85
Cornell University, 171, 185
Countryside radio programme, 108–9, 168, 172, 184, 186
coypu, 168
crake: black, 153; little, 115
Cramp, Stanley, 181
crane, Florida sandhill, 45
Crawley, John, 176
crocodile, 105, 146, 149, 153
crossbill, 96, 109, 116; Scottish, 99
Crosland, Anthony, 139
crow, pied, 143
cuckoo, 91, 119; great spotted, 118, 122; yellow-billed, 175
curlew, 97; stone, 95–6, 109, 116
Curran, Sir Charles, 128

Dalyell, Tam, 130
Darlow, George, 82
Daunt, Michael, 58–9
De Manio, Jack, 48, 141
Deane, Jones, Idris, 28, 29
Deer: Bawean, 166; fallow, 84, 121, 171; red, 101, 136, 137, 174; Sika 171
Dempsey, Gen. Sir Miles, 78
dik-dik, 158
dikkop, water, 153
Dimbleby, Richard, 94, 111
dipper, black-bellied, 93
Dollis Hill, 129, 131, 140–2, 144–5, 176, 177, 183, 184
dotterel, 98–9
Dougall, Robert, 109–10, 128, 131

Douglas-Home, Henry, 92, 129
dove: ground, 45; mourning, 45; red-eyed, 150; rock, 86, 120; stock, 24
Drabble, Phil, 178
Driberg, Tom, 127
duck: ferruginous, 122; maccoa, 160; tufted, 180; wood, 46; yellow-billed, 160
Dungeness, 103–4
dunlin, 97, 98

eagle: bald, 45; Bateleur, 149; black-chested, 149; booted, 118; fish, 150, 151, 153; golden, 99–101, 174; martial, 149; short-toed, 118; tawny, 160; Verraux's, 160; Wahlberg's, 149
Eckersley, Timothy, 90
Ega, Hussein, 147, 148, 156, 157, 161, 162
egret: American, 45; cattle, 121, 122, 149; little, 115, 122, 148; white, 153
eland, 156, 159
elephant: African, 150, 151–2, 153, 154, 161, 162, 165; Indian, 104
Ellis, E. A. (Ted), 93, 168, 178
Ellison, Norman ('Nomad'), 93
Elwell, Felicia, 11, 110, 124–5, 132, 135, 138, 177
Everard, Peter, 83–4
Everglades, 45, 48, 166
Eyre, Ronald, 125

Fair Isle, 109, 129–30, 136, 171, 185
Farne Islands, 34, 101–3, 109, 185
Fawdry, Kenneth, 125, 139
Ferris, Paul, 109
fieldfare, 91, 93, 131
film direction, 96, 106, 125–6, 127, 132–9
finch: Darwin's, 167; fire, 163; snow, 143
firecrest, 104, 171
Fisher, James, 92, 121, 125, 172, 185
Fitter, R. S. R., 24, 131
flamingo: greater, 13–15, 116, 143, 148, 160, 179; lesser, 148
flycatcher: crested, 45; pied, 42; red-breasted, 97
fox: bat-eared, 162; flying, 170; red, 121, 174, 178
France, 60, 76–8, 114–16, 177, 179
Freeman, Sgt W. (Bill), 58, 68, 69, 70, 72
Frontiers for Man, 130, 185
fulmar, 36, 86, 135
Futehally, Zafar, 165

Index

gallinule, purple, 46
Gandhi, Mrs Indira, 169
gannet, 36, 130
garganey, 83, 96
gazelle: Grant's, 158, 160;
  Thomson's, 156, 158, 159, 160, 162
genet, 121, 152
George, R. V. A. (Brian), 88, 110
gerenuk, 162
giraffe, 148, 159, 162
Glover, C. Gordon, 108, 177
Gold, Jack, 127
goldcrest, 99, 100, 103
goldeneye, 97, 181
Gomes, Don José Antonio Valverde, 116–17
goosander, 99
goose: Brent, 97, 98; Canada, 93; Chinese, 129; Egyptian, 93, 151; grey lag, 180; pink-footed, 93, 180; white-fronted, 93, 103
Gordon, Jeanne (sister-in-law) 59, 85, 142, 146
goshawk, 117
grackle, boat-tailed, 46
Grant, Lt-Col J. P., 99
Grattan, Donald, 125
grebe: great crested, 83, 160; little, 96, 148
Greene, Sir Hugh Carleton, 112
greenshank, 97, 98, 99, 158
Grenfell, Joyce, 176
Grierson, John, 26, 132
Griffith, Kenneth, 85
Grisewood, Freddie, 109, 172, 175
grouse, red, 34, 100, 174
guillemot, 86, 101
guinea-fowl, helmeted, 156
gull: Bonaparte's, 46; grey-headed, 161; herring, 39, 40, 86; laughing, 46

Haldane, Prof J. B. S., 25, 117
Hall-Craggs, Joan, 172, 175
harrier, marsh, 83, 96, 115, 137; Montagu's, 83, 121, 137, 151; pallid, 151
Harris, Marshal of the RAF Sir Arthur, 60, 64, 65, 78, 80
Harrisson, Prof. T. H., 166, 169
hartebeest, Jackson's, 150
Harwood, George, 20, 24
hawk: duck, 45; Cooper's, 51; red-tailed, 45
Hawkins, Desmond, 108, 172
Haynes, Grp Capt. Philip, 57–60, 62, 64, 65, 72, 73, 77, 78–9
hedgesparrow, 171

Heralds of the Dawn, 92
heron: goliath, 153; green-backed, 158; grey, 102, 122; little blue, 48; Louisiana, 48; night, 48, 115, 122; purple, 83, 115, 122; squacco, 115
Hewer, Prof. Humphrey, 95, 127
Hilbre Islands, 93, 94, 184
hippopotamus, 149, 151, 152, 153, 160
Hitler, Adolf, 22, 68, 77, 95
hobby, 29
Hoffman, Dr Luc, 116, 168
hog, giant forest, 146
Holland, 83, 177, 186
Hollom, P. A. D. (Phil), 24
Home, Lilian Dowager Countess of, 92–3
hoopoe, 118
Hopkins, Ian, 168
hornbill, ground, 151
Hosking, Eric, 11, 91, 93, 94, 121
hummingbird, ruby-throated, 45
Hurcomb, Lord, 113, 181
Huxley, Sir Julian, 89, 113
hyaena, spotted, 152, 157, 158–9, 160, 165
hyrax, rock, 157–8

ibex, alpine, 144
ibis: African wood, 153; glossy, 155; hadada, 151; Japanese crested, 169; sacred, 148, 161; wood, 45, 48
impala, 148, 154, 156, 162
Insect World, The, 128, 185
Italy, 143, 146, 185, 186
Ivanov, A. I., 117

jackals, 160
jackdaw, 93
Jackson, Charles (father-in-law), 73, 140, 142
jaguar, 104,
James, David Lloyd, 109
jay, 23, 24
Jellis, Rosemary, 175
Johnson, E. D. H., 92
Johnston, Brian, 92
Jones, Derek, 141, 176
Jones, Oliver Graham, 104–5
Journey into Spring, 110–11

Kenya, 82, 113, 147–9, 155–6, 162–3,
kestrel, 176; lesser, 120
killdeer, 45
kingfisher, 23, 96; malachite, 151; pied, 153; woodland, 154
Kirby, John, 92, 171
kite: African black, 147, 155; black, 118, 122; swallow-tailed, 48

Index

kittiwake, 86, 101, 135
Knight, Maxwell, 94-5, 127, 129
knot, 94, 97
kob, Uganda, 150
Koch, Dr Ludwig, 89, 90, 91-2, 172
Kruuk, Dr Hans, 158, 165

Laflin, Kenneth and Monica, 32, 135
Lagus, Charles, 35-7, 138
lammergeier, 122-3
Lang, Dr Ernst, 117, 169
langur, golden, 166
lapwing, 103; crowned, 158
lark: flappet, 158; red-capped, 158; shore, 97; short-toed, 118
Lawley, Sue, 178
Leakey, Dr Louis, 159
Leon, Judge H. C., 142
leopard, 158, 160, 161
lilytrotter, 151
limpkin, 45
lion: African, 104, 105, 153, 154, 157, 159, 160, 162; Asiatic, 165
Lofthouse, William, 84, 87
London Natural History Society, 24, 93, 140, 184
Longmore, Air Chief Marshal Sir Arthur, 79
Love, Enid, 125
lynx, 121; caracal, 104

McAfee, Dr Grant, 93
MacGregor, Sue, 178
MacNiece, Louis, 112
McWhinnie, Donald, 126
magistracy, 144-5, 185
magpie, 171; azure-winged, 122
mallard, 83, 122
Mammals in Britain, 127, 185
Manson-Bahr, Sir Philip, 112
marmot, alpine, 143-4
Marre, Dr Leonard, 141
Martin, Brian, 179
Martin, Dr R. D. (Bob), 165, 169
martin: African sand, 149; crag, 120; house, 86, 140
Masterpieces of Bird Recording, 92
Matthews, Dr L. Harrison, 127, 169
Maxted, Stanley, 110
Meinertzhagen, Col. Richard, 21-2, 112, 122-3, 146
merlin, 29
Merton College, 22, 26, 27-31, 33-4, 38, 81, 112, 184
Miles, Dame Margaret, 173
Minsmere, 95-6, 103, 137-8, 168,
Mirzoeff, Edward, 141
mockingbird, 46

monitor, Nile, 153
Montgomery, F/M Lord, 78, 94
moorhen, 115, 149
Mountfort, Guy, 121, 166, 168
Muggeridge, Douglas, 165
Mulligan, Geoffrey, 129, 137-8, 176
Mylne, Christopher, 129

Nathan, Alfred, 21
Neal, Dr Ernest, 95, 127, 129, 178
Neilson, S/Ldr J. D., 64, 67, 68, 69, 70, 71, 72, 73, 75, 77, 78
Nethersole-Thompson, Desmond, 98
Nicholson, E. M., 24, 89
nightingale, 24, 115, 118
nightjar, 106
Norris, C. A., 85
North, M. E. W. (Myles), 113
Northey, Peter, 146, 149, 151

ocelot, 104
Oman, Julia Trevelyan, 127-8
O'Meara, Sgt Kevin, 58, 68, 69
orang-outang, 104-5, 166
oribi, 150
oriole, golden, 117, 119
oryx, fringe-eared, 162
osprey, 136, 137-8, 168
ostrich, 158, 159, 160, 161
owl: barn, 135; burrowing, 45; eagle, 120; little, 29; Scops, 115; short-eared, 29; tawny, 24, 93
Oxford, 16, 18, 22, 26, 27-34, 38, 59, 60, 80, 81, 170
oxpecker, 162
oystercatcher, 86, 98

Palmér, Sture, 90, 170
Parrinder, E. R., 24, 90-1, 93, 109
partridge, red-legged, 32, 119
pelican: African white, 148; American white, 46; brown, 48
penguin: Adelie, 170; chinstrap, 170; jackass, 129
peregrine, 36, 98, 109, 118
Perry, Roger, 92, 167, 171
Peterson, Roger Tory, 93, 116, 121
Philip, Prince, 92, 93, 169, 175
Phillips, Arthur, 109, 110
Phillips, Flt-Lt. H. B., 60, 67, 68
Pickstock, Michael, 164-5
pipit: meadow, 140, 176; Richard's 158; rock, 86; water, 96
plover: blacksmith, 148; Caspian, 158; golden, 98, 103; grey, 97; Kittlitz's sand, 148; little ringed, 90-1, 109; ringed, 98

Index

pochard: common, 180; red-crested, 83; southern, 148, 160
polecat, 121
Poore, Dr Duncan, 166
pratincole, white-collared, 154
ptarmigan, 100, 137
puffin, 86, 101
pupfish, Devil's Hole, 166

RAF, 29, 35–8, 40, 41, 43–8, 49–50, 53–80, 83–4, 130, 184
rail, water, 115
raven, 120, 143; fan-tailed, 157
Rawcliffe, Donald, 28, 29, 81
Rawlings, Marjorie Kinnan, 44–48
razorbill, 86
recording wildlife, 14–15, 88–107, 109, 112, 114–23, 138, 167, 170, 171–2, 179, 180
redshank, 83, 96; spotted, 96
reedbuck, 158
Reid, Robert, 110
Return to the Camargue A, 179
rhinoceros, black, 156, 160, 161, 162; Indian, 165
Rippon, Geoffrey, 181
Robb, Maj. Eustace, 134
Roberts, S/O Kay, 59
robin: European, 89, 103; American, 40; red-backed scrub, 152
robin-chat, white-browed, 156
Rogers, Harold, 111
roller, 119; lilac-breasted, 162
Rountree, S/O Lynda, 79
Royal Society for the Protection of Birds, 95–6, 110, 113, 181, 184, 185
ruff, 158

St Kilda, 52, 129–30
Sankey, John, 127
sandpipers, 46, 83, 97, 98, 148, 153
Saul, Patrick, 112
scoter, common, 171
Scott, Sir Peter, 93, 151, 168, 169, 173
Scottish Highlands, 98–101, 124, 168, scrub-bird, noisy, 169
seal, grey, 102–3, 130, 135
secretary bird, 156, 158
Selborne, 23, 110–11
Sellar, Patrick, 171–2, 175
serin, 118, 119, 142
shag, 86, 101, 135
shama, white-rumped, 89
Sheffield, Margaret (Meg), 173–4
shelduck, 96, 98
shoveler, 83, 160

shrike: fiscal, 147; woodchat, 119, 122
Simms, Amanda Jane (daughter), 130, 142–3, 146, 174, 183, 185, 186
Simms, Amy Margaret (mother), 16, 18–20, 27, 30, 33–4, 55, 81, 127, 181, 185
Simms, David Barford (son), 130, 142–3, 146, 174, 183, 185
Simms, Levi (father), 16, 19, 20, 26, 32–3, 35, 81, 127, 181, 185
Simms, Margaret Amy (Mrs Deryck Winterton, sister), 18, 19, 81, 181
Simms, Thelma (wife), 11–12, 59, 60, 65, 71, 72–3, 76, 79, 80, 81, 84, 85, 113, 117, 129, 141–3, 146–63, 170, 176, 184
Simms, Thomas Henry (brother), 18, 19–20, 21, 22, 28, 32, 81, 82, 83, 105, 112, 181
Simms, Wilfrid Burgess (brother), 11, 17, 18, 19, 21, 22–3, 28, 81, 112, 181
Simon, Noel, 168
Singleton, Jack, 164
Sitwell, Nigel, 166
Skempton, Alan, 36, 50
skuas, 36, 39, 136, 170, 171
skylark, 32, 103, 135, 140
Sladen, Dr W. J. L. (Bill), 170
snipe, 98, 102
Snow, Dr David, 166
Songs and Calls of British Birds, The, 113, 185
Sorensen, Jeremy, 168
Spain, 25, 117–23
sparrow: house, 86; rock, 118
spoonbill, 82, 122; African, 161; roseate, 48
starling, 85, 86, 96, 102, 103, 140, 176; blue-eared glossy, 154; superb, 157
Stibbe, Philip, 28, 81
stilt: black-necked, 46; black-winged, 115, 116, 148, 179
stint, little, 148, 161
stork: marabou, 148, 151, 158; openbill, 153, 155; saddle-billed, 150; white, 120, 121, 156, 158, 159
Street, Denys, 35
Strijbos, J. P., 83
sunbird: amethyst, 148; golden-winged, 161; variable, 148
Sutton, Graham and Shaun, 23
swallow: European, 135, 140, 148; striped, 149; wire-tailed, 153
swan, whooper, 168, 180
swift, 92, 135; alpine, 120
swiftlet, cave, 166

Index

Switzerland, 116–17, 141–2, 143–4, 146, 185, 186

Tanzania, 156–62
teal, 29, 83, 99
tern: Arctic, 101–2; black, 83; common, 46; Forster's, 46; little, 46, 96; royal, 46
Thorpe, Prof. W. H., 106
thrush: rock, 120; song, 38, 103; wood, 40
tiger, 101
tit: bearded, 96; blue, 18, 177; coal, 143; crested, 119, 143; great, 143; marsh, 24; penduline, 115, 116
titmouse, tufted, 46
Tombs, David, 179
Toovey, Barry, 127
topi, 156, 158
Torday, Emil, 146
Tredwin, F/O R. H. T. (Dick), 58 68, 69, 70, 75, 76
Tucker, Bernard, 28
Tweedie, Michael, 166
twite, 34

Uganda, 149–55, 185
underwater recording, 105–6, 185
United States, 40–53, 170, 175, 182
University College, Oxford, 27, 29, 30–1, 33
University of London, 26, 112–13
Unwin, Stanley, 85, 90, 126–7

Vaughan-Thomas, Wynford, 109, 110
Veprintsev, Boris, 117
vicuna, 167
Vincent, Col Jack, 168
Voices of the Wild, 11, 95, 106, 185
vulture: American black, 45; black, 121; Egyptian, 118, 120, 160; griffon, 120, 121; hooded, 158; turkey, 45; white-backed, 154, 160

Wade, G. F. (Bob), 94, 95, 96–8, 99–104, 105, 114–18, 120–2, 124
wagtail: African white, 147; grey, 99; pied, 99, 176; Spanish, 119
wallcreeper, 120
Warwick, Alex, 130, 136
warbler: Bonelli's, 142; Cetti's, 114, 115, 118; grasshopper, 106; great reed, 83, 113, 122; melodious, 115, 119; moustached, 114; reed, 24, 83, 96, 122; Sardinian, 122; Savi's, 122; sedge, 24; spectacled, 114; subalpine, 122; willow, 38
Ward, Peter, 134–5
waterbuck, 153, 161
warthog, 150, 156
waxwing, 168, 171
Wayre, Philip, 165–6, 169
weaver, grey-headed, 157; Taveta golden, 162
Weismann, Carl, 170
Wellings, Bob, 178
Welsh Harp Conservation Group, 180, 186
wheatear, 103, 148, 166; black, 120
Whittle, Air Cmdr Sir Frank, 58, 84
wigeon, 29, 93, 180; cape, 148
wildebeest, 156, 157, 158, 159, 160
Wildlife Records, BBC, 168–9, 172
Wild Life in the Royal Parks, 181, 186
Wildfowl Trust, The, 32, 103, 173, 184
Wilkinson, F. W., 25
Williamson, Kenneth, 175
Willis, Douglas, 168
Wilson, John, 168
Wilson, Mary, 136
Winterton, Deryck (brother-in-law), 81–2, 88
Witherby's Sound Guide to British Birds, 113, 185
Woman's Hour, 109–10, 178
Wood, S. C. (Stanley), 21, 25
woodcock, 102
Woodland Birds, 82, 172, 186
Woodlark, 119
woodpecker: great spotted, 23, 24; green, 24, 118–19; middle spotted, 117; red-bellied, 45
World Wildlife Fund, 165, 168
wren: Carolina, 45; Fair Isle, 136, 171–2

Year in the Country, A, 134, 135, 185
Year's Journey, A, 138, 172, 177–8, 185
Yeates, G. K. (George), 23, 96–7, 114

zebra, Burchell's, 156, 158, 159, 160
zoos, 35, 105–6, 111, 117, 184
Zoo Quest, 111, 135, 138